Mr. F.O'K.

A True Story

Elena PM

Mr. F.O'K.

ISBN 13 - 978-1539675501
LCCN: 2016498027

"And I don't see why I should spend my life trying to prove anything to anyone"

- Francis O'Keefe, Jr.

Acknowledgments

I offer a big "Thank You" to the following persons:

Pedro A. Yanes is one of those "forever" friends who encouraged me from day one to set down on paper the life of Francis O'Keefe, Jr.

Osmel Hogen (1939-2015) has my eternal gratitude for transferring Francis's words and songs from cassettes onto CDs so that they may remain safe.

Margaret Rose Scribner is a fine artist and ghost writer who taught me a lot about self-publishing.

Ernesto Contenti, a long time friend who downloaded for me the publishing template used to put this book into its final format and helped me with other computer issues.

Kristen Sternberg, a copy editor who lent advice about the book's readability and did an excellent job correcting my grammatical errors. Also, as I sent her the chapters she always had words of praise for my narrative which I really appreciated.

Many thanks to Elizabeth Ehrnst from the Georgia O'Keeffe Museum and to Melissa Barton from Beinecke Library at Yale University for all their assistance and their patience with my ignorance on issues of copyrights.

Prologue

I'm not a professional writer. I'm going to tell, using my own words, photographs, documents, and the times we shared, the true story of Francis O'Keefe, Jr.

Our paths crossed and with the passing of the days I came to know, respect and love this homeless man whom many branded as lazy or crazy, and in whom I discovered a noble, intelligent, educated and talented man with an exquisite sense of humor.

He is homeless. Like so many others that abound and roam all the cities of the world.

He is one of many who, at a crucial time in their lives, did not or could not make decisions that would lead them to a healthier and more dignified way of life.

Francis, an aristocratic indigent.
Indigent by circumstances of life.
Aristocratic by his own nature.

Table of Contents

<u>Homeless.</u>

Early one Monday morning in April of 1998, I arrived at WDR Library as a newly-hired assistant librarian, fully confident of my ability to do a good job.

As always, when I undertake something new, I was exalted with curiosity, wondering which new experiences and friends this new job would bring to my life.

After my first few days on the job, I began to recognize frequent users of the library, including a white man of medium height, thin and bald, with gray hair and blue eyes. He looked to be about 55 years old, and was poorly dressed; some days scruffier than others.

My co-workers, some derisively, some with indifference, yet others with more pious gestures informed me that he was a homeless man who had been around for the last two years. I began to greet him with a simple "good morning."

One day he approached me and, in a quiet, pleasant and perfect Spanish, without an accent denoting ethnicity, introduced himself as Francis O'Keefe and then asked my name. He then asked, "Would you have a fountain pen I could borrow?"

Not an ordinary pen, no: He needed a fountain pen. I smiled and told him I couldn't help him. He went on to explain that he wrote many letters and they were only readable by using that type of pen. I remembered that I had a Parker at home. I didn't offer it to him, not that day, not ever. And here is that pen languishing without ever having been used.

On one occasion we were at the front of the library next to the stairs and Francis, upon seeing me smoking, asked me for a cigarette.

This would be the first of many that we would share. A few days later I came up with a system that he quickly picked up: I would go out for a smoke, consuming only half of the cigarette and would then leave the other half on the third step. When he felt the urge to smoke, he always knew where to find half a cigarette.

1

When we estimated that each cigarette cost me 15 cents, then the cost of what he smoked was about 7.5 cents. Once a co-worker was surprised to hear Francis ask me for seven and a half cents.

As the days went by I learned that Francis actually lived in the park that surrounds the library, which is ironically called:

I watched Francis from a distance as he went in and out of the library, sometimes talking to an acquaintance, leaving and returning on his bike, sitting always at the same desk and writing or drawing incessantly. I also watched him standing outside while talking to himself.

One very warm morning I saw him arrive with a jacket on. Enrique, one of the guards, seeing my expression of surprise asked me, "Do you know what that is? That's hunger. When one is hungry, one feels cold." I do not remember what I thought, or whether I managed to coordinate any thoughts at all. I know I felt BADLY. Yes, with capital letters.

An hour later, in the dining room of the library, with a plate of chicken, rice and salad in front of me, despite my appetite, I could barely eat. In my mind was engraved the image of this man with an expression of weariness in his face, walking with his hands inside the pockets of his jacket and Enrique's voice saying, "That's Hunger!"

Hurriedly, I ate a little and with more than half of my lunch, I went in search of Francis.

That day I made my debut in the underworld of the homeless existence.

From that day on, I began to arrive at the library an hour earlier provided with a bag of clothes, biscuits, boiled eggs (his favorite dish), razor blades and so on.

At that time in 1998, on my sole salary I had to maintain my own house, two dogs, and a yellow compact car, along with my overhead. So, I started "begging" friends and family for used men's clothes and other things I felt could be useful to Francis. One afternoon he said, "I have come to think that only people who wear big sizes are charitable." He was a medium, but I had managed to get him only large shirts and sweaters.

I had noticed that Francis wore a pair of dilapidated brown boots, which he told me were extremely heavy. One day, while at a gathering of about 20 family members and friends at my brother Carlos's home, I asked them to give me a dollar each to buy a pair of shoes for Francis. The looks I got in return I could not even decipher: they were a mixture of pity, sarcasm and I don't know what else. No one cooperated. As I was leaving, my brother gave me a twenty-dollar bill.

The next morning I arrived at the library with new shoes, size 8½, and a pair of socks. Francis received these gifts with great joy. Instantly, he put the new shoes on and said: "What a relief I feel! I have been suffering from tremendous pain in my back and it has almost disappeared." Seeing him barefoot I noticed that his feet were clean and without calluses, and that his nails were properly clipped. Now, seeing him clean-shaven wearing new shoes, I said, "Now all you need is cologne."

"Guerlain, of course," was his answer.

I was surprised. I have to admit having had prejudiced thoughts at that moment. Here was a homeless man talking about classic and expensive perfumes. Shame on me. I knowing well that appearances can be deceiving. Since I was 11 years old I've used only Shalimar. Francis liked the essence of Heure Bleu. So, our conversation went on about Guerlain. That day after experiencing his good manners, his most correct Spanish and English and the perfumed conversation, I said, "You know, Francis, you have class." He replied with a big smile, "Finally someone recognizes it!" And he extended his hand to me.

The week of Memorial Day I had the weekend and Monday off. On Sunday at noon I was heading for a family lunch and could not help but stray toward the library as I imagined how bored and possibly hungry Francis would be.

About three blocks from the park I spotted him riding his bike. I blew the horn of my car and signaled that I was waiting for him. That day I took my first pictures of him.

He showed me what we baptized as "the apartment," a site close to an eight-foot high wall separating the park from an apartment building. There, in plastic buckets, he kept his things: clothes, bike tools, drawings, and writings and more writings. I offered to put some order among his things and ended up in a nearby laundry washing and drying his rusty and poor clothes. From there we went to a supermarket where I bought him a few things to eat.

That day I arrived at the family lunch at time for dinner, but happy with myself for all that I had accomplished for Francis. My family patiently listened to my story and, as so often, I heard them say, "She is crazy!"

Francis received about $100 in food stamps on the 2nd day of ever-month, but without a place to store or cook food, everything he bought had to be consumed daily. They were always cold things: milk, fruits, bread, canned meat and candy. Around the 21st day he would have already spent the money and then he depended on what someone cared to give him. Once in a while he stopped at Taco Bell, where they would give him two free burritos.

It was about a month after I met him that I learned about this.

I offered to bring to my house about $60 dollars of groceries bought with his food-stamps. I then could bring him a daily meal I prepared; nothing "gourmet" because I barely know how to boil water, but definitely a meal superior to what he had been consuming.

Later, I also volunteered to do his laundry at my house.

Practically speaking, I became Mr. O'Keefe's servant, chauffeur, cigarette provider and a friend to whom he could talk.

Francis's Personality

1998 at WDR

I began to spend more time after working hours with Francis.

We would drive to buy snacks and then come back to the park, where we would settle on a bench or on the stairs to eat, drink café/leche, smoke, chat and listen to music. We enjoyed these gatherings countless times.

Francis was a charismatic man, partly thanks to his physical appearance: thin with gray hair, delicate features and those blue eyes with their steady look. He had the talent to make a fun story from the simplest tale and his laughter was contagious. His conversation in both languages (English and Spanish) was very correct.

Also, as I noted on many occasions, he had great powers of observation or what is called a photographic memory. I remember the first time he got in my car and, after fastening his seat belt, he asked if he could turn the radio on. Francis instantly found the right buttons for volume and to change the stations. Maybe I am dazed, but when I bought my car it took me half an hour to understand the radio controls as well as the air-conditioning system. Francis captured everything in a minute.

I came to believe that either I had atrophied senses or Francis was highly charged. He perceived faint odors in the environment, distinguished small flowers in the grass and heard sounds that I could barely detect but were actually there.

Francis liked classical music, understood it and enjoyed it. One of his favorite composers was Gustav Mahler. He was also a connoisseur of Cuban and Latin popular music in general. During our meetings, I often asked him to sing, for he had a warm and smooth voice, which I recorded several times onto a portable cassette player. Every time I hear *Habanera Tu or You are my Sunshine*, I think of him.

The first joke he told me was as follows:

"How do we define the different states of sexual potency through classical music?"

The impotent ----------Tocatta and Fugue ------------by Bach	
The semi-impotent ----The Unfinished Symphony ---by Schubert	
The powerful ------------------The 9 Symphonies --------by Beethoven	
The super powerful -----------The Firebird --------------by Stravinsky	

At times Francis looked lost; in his mind other thoughts or voices arose that made him smile or gesture. At first I was a little afraid, but I got used to it, because his behavior was never aggressive. I had to bring him back. "Francis, Francis: Are you here?"

"Yes, I'm back," was his usual reply.

Once he explained, as a joke, the three stages of talking to oneself:
1 - When you only speak.
2 - When you speak and you answer.
3 - When you speak and ask yourself, "What?"

Honesty

Diogenes, the Greek philosopher, would have stopped looking for an honest man if he had known Francis. One incident touched me deeply and showed the degree of honesty of this man. One afternoon I was working at the Reference desk when Francis approached and handed me a wallet he had found lying around. It contained identifications and about $100 in cash.

I informed my supervisor. We contacted the owner, who came within an hour to pick it up. I asked him to verify the contents.

"Yes," he said, "it's all here, thank you very much."

I said, "No sir, do not thank me. Do you see that gentleman who is sitting on a bench outside? It was he who found it. His name is Francis and he is homeless."

The man was stunned. Upon leaving, he stopped where Francis was and gave him $20. That night, Francis paid for the *café con leche.*

Stoicism

When Francis suffered a mishap - misplaced something, the bike broke down, or he was a victim of abuse; under no circumstance did he react rudely. If it was in his hands to confront the aggressor or to report abuse, he did not hesitate to do so; otherwise, with a shrug, he would say in Spanish-Cuban, *"me chivé / me chivaron"* (*chivar*: to lose or abuse) and would not allow the incident to spoil the rest of his day. Also, his complaints were mild when feeling physical pain, no matter how strong, as we would discover years later.

Chivalry

An absolute gentleman: that is what Francis was. I will never forget the first time, after our first evening reunion, when Francis walked me to my car and opened the driver's door for me. Then, there was the time we went to a Burger King and Francis, after carrying our tray to a table, waited for me to sit down first. Then, after sitting across from me, he unfolded a napkin and placed it on his lap. Opening doors for people, picking up someone's keys from the floor, saying "please" and "thank you" were part of Francis's natural behavior.

Cursing was absolutely non-existent in Francis's vocabulary. I remember with humor an incident that made me feel as *Dulcinea.* Francis and I were sitting on the stairs outside the library when there came along an acquaintance who began to chat with Francis using some bad words. For him they were part of his vocabulary but not for Francis, who immediately said to him, "I will not allow you to speak like that in the presence of this lady."

The man, who was shorter than Francis but younger and stockier, gaped for a few seconds, then apologized. The conversation ended there. Francis stood up and said, "Let's go."

And *Dulcinea* left accompanied by *Don Quixote.*

How Does One Live On the Streets?

Answering this question would take another book. It would require the participation of professionals: social workers, policemen, doctors, etc. There are many factors that vary by individual. The streets of New York, Los Angeles, Houston or Miami, to name a few cities, are not the same for an indigent person for reasons of climate and the attitudes of the local citizenry and authorities. The media have often exposed stories and videos showing public abuses and even deaths inflicted upon the homeless. Other factors that can make a difference are the physical appearance, race, age, behavior and pathological state of the individual. And definitely the most important factor is the cause of the situation: drug addiction, alcoholism, mental illness, and many other ailments that can intrude into and destroy a life.

These are my own conclusions, but I am not an expert and I'm not going to continue discussing this topic.

As to how Francis lived on the streets for nearly 20 years, I can speak with authority and offer details. Especially since that April of 1998 when I met him until the day he left prison in August 1999, and I brought him to live at my house.

Nights in Miami can be hot, humid and full of mosquitoes. Though its winter nights are the mildest in the nation, they offer no relief when it comes to spending them poorly-fed, poorly-wrapped and sleeping on a concrete floor, beneath a stairwell or on a park bench. Let's add to it that Francis could have been attacked by a rat or a thug.

In the mornings, wherever he had spent the night, he needed to pick up his things at daybreak to avoid being seen and exposing his night-time hiding place.

His physiological needs had to be attended to by going into the bushes or using public restrooms at a McDonald's or similar establishment.

Personal hygiene was resolved in different ways. Among his possessions were soap, toothbrush, toothpaste, deodorant and a razor. After 11 at night, when everyone had left the park, he would open with a clip the taps located at the side of the library building and fill a bucket with water. Then, hidden and wearing only a bathing trunks, he bathed. Besides the fear of being seen, there were the mosquitoes, the midnight cold (even in Miami), and a cold water bath will give anyone goose bumps.

Matheson Park, located about 12 miles south of WDR, has among other amenities a beach and public showers. And from time to time Francis pedaled his bike up there to enjoy a double feature: sea and shower. In his visits to the park he also enjoyed the landscape and its residents: iguanas, land crabs, raccoons, birds, etc. Furthermore, it was not unusual for him to share a conversation with another person and be invited for snacks.

WDR library opened Monday through Thursday from 9:30 a.m. to 9 p.m. and Friday and Saturday 9:30 a.m. to 6:00 p.m. It offered Francis during those hours protection from high and low temperatures and rainy days. There he could read, write, use the public bathrooms and treat himself to a nap in one of the armchairs. The latter is not allowed in public libraries but, Francis was always discreet and behaved correctly; and just in case I was watchful.

" I conceived that those in beggary are in that state against their will, for there is not a philosophy by which someone may desire to live in beggary, the existentialists, the hippies, having each a philosophy by which they live or lived, but a philosophy to live in beggary does not exist."
- *Francis O'Keefe,Jr.*

A Bicycle Called "la Niña"

The bike was his most prized possession, his means of transportation and a favorite topic of conversation.

I'm not a cyclist. I thought that a bicycle consisted only of a horse with two wheels, a seat, pedals and steering. I assumed there were different manufacturers and prices. Ah, but after meeting Francis I came to believe they were more complicated and more expensive than a fighter aircraft. Different designs of handlebars and seats, tires with varying air pressure, chains, ball cages, rear and front headlights, hand or pedal brakes, bells, mirrors and many other components.

It is also advisable to dismantle one's bike every so many miles to wash all the mechanisms, oil and re-assemble them. Then there are many different security locks to prevent theft when parked. Also there are a dozen models of helmets for cyclists.

To ride his bike efficiently, Francis carried in his backpack an air pump, patches and various tools. Despite so much knowledge and care the bike was always in need of something. I came to think that Francis himself was breaking it, so to have something to complain about and later to be occupied with. It had a flat tire almost every day. How could that be possible?

One day the bike had so many problems that Francis was depressed. I promised him that after work I would take the "wounded" bicycle in my car/ambulance to the repair shop/hospital where he and his bike were both known; trusting that it was not going to be a very expensive affair.

The owners of "Bird Road Cycle World", a family of Chinese origin, treated Francis with much consideration. While the bike was being repaired, Francis gave me a "tour" of the store, explaining differences between one bicycle and another. He felt like a fish in water. Once his bike was fixed, Francis was a happy camper and I went home.

Parked in front of WDR

Ready to go

The next morning, as soon as I saw Francis, I asked him in Spanish, "How is the girl (la niña)?"
"What girl?" he asked.
"What else? The bicycle."
"Oh! Fine, there she is sunbathing."

The Wheels.

Elena's Bicycle

Francis, thanks to his affable nature and to his bike, which he rode all over town, was known by few people who treated him kindly. Such was the case with Mr. Mora, who, in a van parked behind St. Agatha School, received donations - clothing, toys, furniture and almost anything. These donations he gave free of charge to anyone who came in need. A real Goodwill – not like one of those profitable stores.

One afternoon, Francis walked to Mr. Mora's and came back happily riding a different bicycle. That one was a gift for me. During my lunch time, Francis gave me cycling lessons.

I have to admit that despite all the shocks and blows it was exciting to be able to go forward a bit without losing my balance. Once I rode a few yards, downhill, and I felt a great sense of freedom.

But my bike was not exactly a late model and I never did learn to ride, much to Francis's and my dismay.

Every single time I see someone on a bike I feel sorry for not have learned to ride.

<u>The Internet</u>

Sometime in the month of August, free Internet service was installed in all of Miami-Dade's public libraries. Francis immediately began using these computers and opening email accounts. He managed to have about five accounts. He came up with some passwords that not even the best of hackers could figure out. One that I remember was ALBATROSSE. However, there was one email account which we both started.

Re: your mail Monday, September 14, 1998 3:59 PM

From: "Francis O'Keefe Jr" d059338c@dc.seflin.org

Add sender to Contacts To: "Elena" d058768c@dc.seflin.org

I have kept many of the emails that we exchanged throughout the years.

Regarding computers, I was about as current as I was in cycling: totally lost. Finally we learned, Francis much faster than I. Eventually I got good with some programs, while he surpassed me in a few others.

Dancing Under the Stars

One night, after the library had closed and having shared some snacks, *café con leche* and a cigarette, Francis and I put a Cuban music cassette in the boom-box, and… we danced!

If anyone saw us or not, I could have cared less. I do remember thinking that it seemed to me like a movie: A lady librarian dancing in the middle of the night with a homeless man in the vestibule of the library.

We had a great time though. Francis danced well and we got along as if we had always danced together. It had been over 30 years since the last time he had danced. I was filled with joy to see him so happy.

Dancing Floor

Schizophrenia

> *Schizophrenia is a chronic and severe disorder that affects how a person thinks, feels, and acts. People with the disorder may hear voices or see things that aren't there. They may believe other people are reading their minds, controlling their thoughts, or plotting to harm them. Sometimes the voices talk to each other, and sometimes people with schizophrenia talk to the voices that they hear. – National Institute of Mental Health.*

When he talked about the "pains and voices" in his head I never found an adequate answer to give him; all I was able to do was to listen or try to console him with words: some perhaps silly but always compassionate. What I'm sure of is that my friendship did him good.

One of the fixations he suffered had to do with Josefita (Fita), the family maid who became his nanny. According to him, Josefita (d. 1982) imposed criteria or ill advice upon him.

Here are a few of the hundreds of Francis's statements written in Spanish or English throughout the years, before and after we met.

Unfortunately for most of my life I have been attacked by voices of mob people. They have caused me extensive damage psychosomatic. I have written to powerful people - CEOs of major corporations, politicians, scientists but nobody does anything to understand my malady. And so I live in this undeserved misery.

I discovered that when J. * talks. She removes the power from me to struggle. Today, March 4, 1999, again is that I discovered this. Small, about 4' 5" tall, chubby, mulatto, uneducated, poor, humble gestures and actions to everyone, always willing to do for all, always running for it, Josefita earned many. That Josefita was imposed against me and over me is obvious. And I see no other explanation for all this, all pointing to Josefita, unless that Josefita was who hurt me, knowingly providing all the same.
How did this emerge I do not know.

I can, moreover, hear again what someone has said whose statements are important to me, even after several decades. I can also replay concertos and symphonies perfectly, although not in their entirety, I heard and liked very much. This is excellent memory. I can also create dialogues and hear them spoken, and I can even see, mentally I suppose is the name, what I create, the characters, the scenes, when I wrote short stories.

Years ago, I in beggary, I saw a cloud drawn in a famous painting. It was a fantastic cloud, of many colors, all strong, and I wondered how the painter could have thought of it, and drawn it, perhaps copied it, I now not remembering the question. Next day, or a few days afterwards, I saw exactly the same cloud, the same colors in the same arrangement and the cloud of the same shape, real, in heaven! I was walking down the street and I looked up, and I saw it! So I was called to see it too! And I then ceased to look up, not knowing then and now why, very probably so done to me by that being or beings that did this for me. Thank you, many thanks!

Letter about the pains caused:

I feel cut through the left part of my face. The cut is deep, and not fast. I feel that part pushed, as well as pulled, and as if sucked. The burning sensation spreads slightly now. I am forced to bite very hard, to the pointof breaking molars and teeth.

It is a constant being attacked. I also feel being hit, pulled out, elsewhere. I see and feel these, and I also see and feel of myself, of me that is, taken out and disappearing, harmed, destroyed. I see my childhood so robbed and destroyed.

I see faces and hear voices, which appear to come from those faces I see,but this may be an illusion, for it appears the voices come from elsewhere.Some of the faces are of people I know, others are of unmet people.

I do not understand these pains that have robbed me of a great life.

Note: In Google I found this reference from 1974, written by Francis on the subject of Schizophrenia.
However, I haven't been able to acquire a copy of his essay.

Library of Congress. Copyright Office - An Essay on two proper-ties of archetypes and An Essay on schizophrenia. By Francis Wyckoff O'Keefe. 6 p. C Francis Wyckoff O'Keefe; 18Auq74; A592490.

From: "Francis O'Keefe Jr." <o_francis@hotmail.com>
To: Ovejas9@yahoo.com
Subject: Life lost
Date: Thu, 01 Apr 1999 19:59:30 EST

```
Gentles:

        I had a fantasy which I wish to write to
you. I thought of
myself, now living in the streets for twenty one
years, and being in a
library every day for several years, joking with
one of the young
librarians saying to her "I will propbably be
here longef than you
will." and then the thought that after my death
she would tell others
"There was an old man who lived in the streets
and went to the library
in which I worked every day, for years, until he
died." as an anecdote
that was different and sad.
        It is sad that a life be lost, only such
known about a person.
```

If begging and homelessness were new issues for me, much more so was schizophrenia. I consulted with a few doctors and followed the recommendations they gave me, which today I can admit were wrong. One recommendation was not to get involved with drugs because they had to be highly supervised, if not the results could be serious. This opinion of the doctors were 50/50 true and false.
Today I know that in the specific case of Francis a correct medication would have worked.

"I'm not crazy," he would tell me.

"I did not say you're crazy, but all that mess of voices and visions can be caused by a chemical imbalance in the brain. You know that the human body is just a chemical machine made of hormones, minerals, plasma, neurotransmitters, etc." – was my reply.

"No!" – he answered emphatically.

As happened quite often, he got angry with me for days and even weeks. Reconciliation was always up to me. Why didn't I tell him to get lost?

a) Because, even in a mild state, Francis was a paranoid schizophrenic. He suffered from an illness that was not his fault nor was he responsible for.

b) Because he was an excellent man, with moral values and good manners that nowadays are almost obsolete.

Therefore, I felt great admiration and affection for Francis.

On one occasion Francis was complaining about some mishap, what it was about I can't remember, and I said to him, "But Francis, think of the many people who are in worse condition than you are."

To which he replied, "I know, but that doesn't help me."

It is a simple truth. If one is in pain, knowing that other people may be even dying does not relieve our own pain. So, I have adopted that phrase which always makes me laugh.

Francis O'Keefe, Jr. Artwork

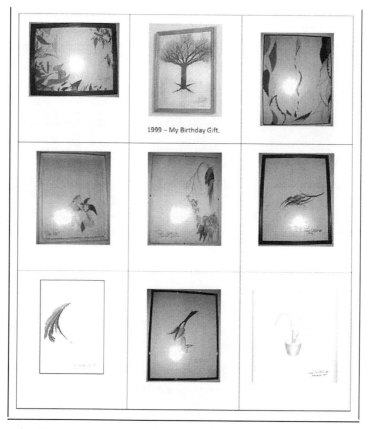

1999 – My Birthday Gift.

Francis liked to sign"*Francis O'Keefe, Jr.*" When a document re-quired it he used "Francis Wyckoff O'Keefe ."

Once I suggested that maybe he should sign as "Francis O'Keefe III" considering that his grandfather and father had the same name: Francis O'Keeffe. His father had removed one "f" from the surname. For a short time he signed some of his drawings as I suggested, but soon returned to his usual identity signature.

"A poem, how difficult it is to write a poem. And I wrote a poem!"

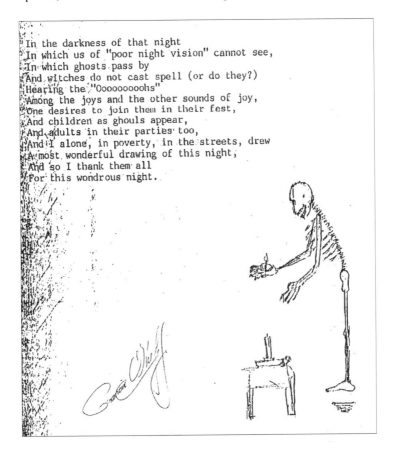

In the darkness of that night
In which us of "poor night vision" cannot see,
In which ghosts pass by
And witches do not cast spell (or do they?)
Hearing the "Ooooooooohs"
Among the joys and the other sounds of joy,
One desires to join them in their fest,
And children as ghouls appear,
And adults in their parties too,
And I alone, in poverty, in the streets, drew
A most wonderful drawing of this night,
And so I thank them all
For this wondrous night.

Here is one of his last drawings: a Chinese teapot, which he was very proud of having done with a Microsoft program in 2008.

O'Keeffe & O'Keefe Families

About two months after our friendship began, one afternoon as we were returning to the library from my break, I asked him casually. "Francis, are you related to Georgia O'Keeffe?"

"Yes, she was my aunt," he replied and kept walking.

My reaction was, "His aunt? What?"

That same day I brought home several biographies of Georgia. And boy! Was I in for a surprise!

Thanks to the fame of his Aunt Georgia, about whom several books have been written, and to the half-million sites online about her, I was able to get data and pictures about his paternal ancestry. In one of the books, I found a genealogy chart in which Francis's name appeared as the last and youngest direct descendant of this O'Keeffe family.

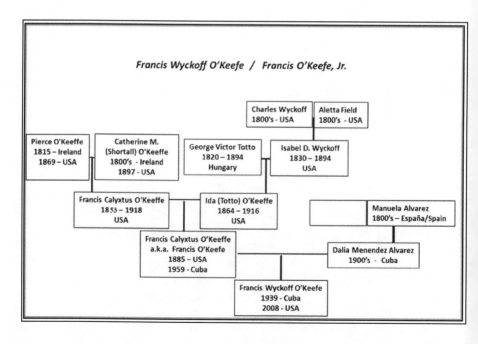

Francis, my homeless and schizophrenic friend, was a descendant of an interesting family.

The life of this man deserved to be told in a book. I told him so, and he replied, "Very well."

From that day on I took notes of his stories and with his authorization I recorded – on tapes – some of our conversations and his "concerts." He loved singing and did it extremely well. He had an enviable pronunciation and intonation.

O'Keeffe and O'Keefe are anglicized versions of the Gaelic surname, Ó Caoimh, from Caomh, meaning "gentle"
- *Wikipedia*

Wyckoff

When the British took over the Dutch colony of New York in 1674, Pieter Claesen adopted the fixed surname of Wyckoff. -
Internet

George Victor Totto (Francis great-grandfather) was born in Hungary.
According to some biographers (see Internet) he was an aristocrat.

Georgia Totto O'Keeffe has been recognized as the "Mother of American modernism."

-Wikipedia

Georgia & Elena

Since the age of 13, when I got my first card from the National Library in Habana, I have not stopped visiting public libraries wherever I've lived - ending as an employee of Miami-Dade Public Library System (1997-2010). Of the hundreds of times I have visited libraries, I have a specific memory of one afternoon, which I guess was in the days of March 1986, with the announcement of Georgia O'Keeffe's death.

I arrived mid-afternoon at SDR library. I went upstairs to where the non-fiction collection and the material in foreign languages are kept. In the middle of the room was a long table with an exhibition of Georgia O'Keeffe's art books and biographies. I stopped to review them and I remember the great paintings of exotic flowers that impacted me. At that time I was unaware of the existence of G.OK, and I was not familiar with the Irish surname O'Keeffe. As a matter of fact, after seeing some photos of her and the name, Georgia O'Keeffe I thought she was a Native American. I had good reasons to think so:

Okefenokee:The largest swamp in North America, the Okefenokee Swamp covers roughly 700 square miles and is located in the southeastern corner of Georgia. The name "Okefenokee" is a Native American word meaning "trembling earth." - nationalgeographic.org/encyclopedia

The name Okeechobee comes from the Hitchiti words oki (water) and chubi (big). - Wikipedia

(2006-06-0793 Unknown photographer - Georgia O'Keeffe in Abiquiu, 1972 -
Color photograph - Gift of the Georgia O'Keeffe Foundation - Georgia O'Keeffe Museum)

What I wonder now is: Why only this memory of the so many times I've visited libraries? A presentiment of what was awaiting me in the future, perhaps?

"I'm the man of coincidences," Francis used to say.

Almost all of us have been surprised by the similarities we have found, with names, numbers, dates, etc. in our lives.

Georgia O'Keeffe was born on November 15, 1887, while I was born on November 15, 1946, 59 years later. Francis was born on February 12, 1939, 51 years after his aunt. When Francis and I met he was 59 years old and I was 51.

After meeting Francis and reading some of Georgia's biographies, I found many similarities in Georgia's and my personalities independently, including both having been born on November 15th and the important events for both of us in 1946.

1946 - The Museum of Modern Art in New York exhibited the works of Georgia O'Keeffe for the first time.

1946 - Georgia widowed by the death of Alfred Stieglitz

1946 - It was the year I was born.

We both have been independent and free-spirited thinkers. Also, simplistic with our wardrobe and foreign to make-up.

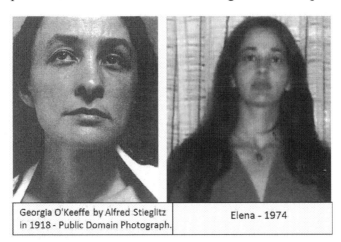

Georgia O'Keeffe by Alfred Stieglitz in 1918 - Public Domain Photograph.

Elena - 1974

Brooklyn Bridge:

I've always loved bridges. I lived for three years in New York in the early 1960s and the bridge I liked the most,of the many that there are in the city, was the Brooklyn Bridge.

Apparently the same happened to Georgia because it was the only one she captured on canvas.

(Georgia O'Keeffe - Brooklyn Bridge - Brooklyn Museum -
Bequest of Mary Childs Draper - No known copyright restrictions.)

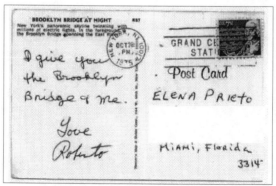

1975 Postcard from a boyfriend

Natural objects:

Georgia was inspired by nature. She collected rocks, dry animal bones, shells. Most of her art work consisted of huge flowers and rough landscapes.

(OB058 - Malcolm Varon -'Lightening' stones and coral pieces, 2001
Copyright Georgia O'Keeffe Museum)

I always have been attracted to dry trees, sea shells, cactus and rocks, the latter are the souvenirs I bring home form my travels.

Jewish:

Alfred Stieglitz (January 1, 1864 - July 13, 1946) was of Jewish origin. He was Georgia artistic promoter, her lover and later her husband

(Alfred-Stieglitz 1902 - Gertrude Kasebier - Public Domain Photograph)

In 1984 the book "Jews, God and History," reached my hands. I read it avidly. Prior to this book I had connected with Jews - friends, employers, boyfriends; but this book opened for me a whole new world.

So much history, traditions, culture! A unique people! Since then I am the "most non-Jewish, yet Jewish person there is" - it's what I answer when I am asked. There is also the possibility of some Jewish blood in me due to my mother's last name: Miranda.

Judaica Collection that I owned till 2013

Nudism:

Georgia allowed herself to be widely photographed nude by Stieglitz.

In 1995, I started going to the only nudist beach that there is in Miami - Halouver Park.
On one occasion I asked a friend to photograph me standing under the shower.

That's how liberal are some of us from November 15!

 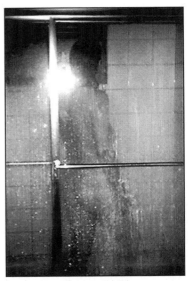

Georgia O'Keeffe A Portrait 1918.
Photographed by Alfred Stieglitz.
Public domain.

Elena – 1995

To conclude with the coincidences between Georgia and me:
Francis O'Keefe, Jr.

The End of 1998

Several months had passed since the beginning of our unique friend-ship as I dealt with what I came to call *perretas,* or "his tantrums." Nonetheless, I kept Francis fed, did his laundry at my house and kept providing the ½ cigarettes. Finally, any given day he was not angry with me anymore. When we were all right, or I should say when he was all right, because I was always fine, then he told me anecdotes of his life. And what a life!

In early November we had in Miami a hurricane warning for the passage of the storm, Mitch. Libraries were not open and I was at home preparing for the storm. I was concerned about Francis but had no idea how to reach him. Around 2 p.m. I turned on the TV and not five minutes had elapsed before they showed one of the shelters and, whom do I see walking with a cup of coffee in hand? Yes, Francis.

As he told me later, he was the first to arrive at the county shelter that was open to those in need. There he met Rita, a very kind Cuban-American lady.

"I met Rita Gomez in a shelter when a hurricane was approaching, she a Red Cross volunteer and in charge of the shelter; I the first to be there."

Thanksgiving Day, as always, I celebrated with my family. Later I phoned Francis at the public phone located right outside of the library entrance. Then, I drove there with his dinner.

At some point I had given him a harmonica, and that night he sur-prised me by playing a few songs.

30

I do not know if the following applies to his extensive knowledge of classical music or to his most excellent memory:

Once, we got into my car and the radio was tuned to a station that transmits only classical music. As Francis turned the radio on, the last notes of a piece were heard, and when I say the last notes I'm saying the last three seconds of the piece: something like tun tun tun. And Francis identified it as "The Four Seasons."

This was corroborated by the announcer a minute later: "We just heard The Four Seasons by Vivaldi."

Once again I looked dumb: I dropped my jaw and, with my mouth open wide, looked at Francis.

Composing a classical music theme: "Here in the apartment, not long ago, I suddenly, trying to compose classical music, did compose. It was only a theme, and it was beautiful! The feeling I felt from doing so was a wonderful one." - *Francis*

Francis was no longer sleeping outdoors; per my suggestion he had begun spending his nights on the covered terrace located on the 2nd floor of the library. There he was much more protected from everything.

This became his new "apartment" while the library was closed.

By then I was familiar with the basic needs of those living in the streets. One evening I went to visit Francis and brought with me a long, wide sheet of plastic. If it rained, he could cover himself or his belongings. Coincidentally, just as I reached the terrace it began to rain heavily and the two of us ended up sitting on the floor and taking refuge under the plastic tent.

Last *perreta/t*antrum of 98:

I do not remember why: it could have been anything I said. According to Francis, I ordered him rather than suggested or asked politely for something. It was my way of speaking, forgetting perhaps to say please. For example, I might say, "Francis, tie the bike now, I'm leaving in five minutes."

Well, Francis had too much character for anyone to order him around.

"When you speak like that I feel a pressure on the right side of the face and it is like I am psychologically being robbed of myself," he told me.

Conclusion: By the last week of the year Francis was angry with me, again! What he did was to ignore and avoid me completely.

December 24th was Thursday and I worked half a day. I waited for the other library employees to leave. Enrique, the security guard, was with me and knew my plan. It consisted of leaving some gifts for Francis on the stairs to his "apartment." Therefore, Enrique invited Francis for coffee at the Latin Cafeteria across the street. Meanwhile I brought the presents and placed them with a sign on the steps. When I saw them coming back I got into my car and left. I knew that Francis was going to be seated alone at the front of the library right by his new space. I waited for about five minutes, then drove back into the area at 45 mph knowing that once he spotted the yellow ball that was my car, he was going to try to get away. I gave him no time for that as I stopped in front of him I said, "Francis, I want to warn you that when you left with Enrique, a white, bearded fat man went up the stairs   of your apartment,   so   please   go   and   check" He only nodded but said nothing. And this time I did go home.

When we met again a few days later, Francis thanked me for the presents and, smiling at me, he stretched out his hand; I went bold and gave him a hug and a kiss on the cheek.

Several times I had wondered: how long has it been since this man does not receive a physical demonstration of affection?

Don't we all – including animals – need that? I mean affection.

Date: Thu, 31 Dec 1998 06:26:53 -0800 (PST)

From: Elena PM epm15@yahoo.com

To: FRANCIS W O'KEEFE

<D059338C@DC.SEFLIN.ORG>

Subject: 1999

Francis, I like to wish you that 1999 be the best year ever of your life. Full of health, joy, $, and peace.
Your friend, always.
Elena

"Feliz Fin de Siglo !!! "

Mr. F.O'K. - Cuban-American

Photo : GENi.com

Francis Calyxtus O'Keeffe – a.k.a. Francis O'Keefe
1885 – Born in Wisconsin, USA

He traveled to Cuba in the 1930's
Architect by profession.
"The Frank Robins building on Obispo was planned by
architect Francis O'Keefe."
On Becoming Cuban: Identity, Nationality, and Culture
By Louis S. Pérez, Jr.

For unknown reasons he changed his name by deleting
his middle name and removing one "f" from O'Keeffe.

In 1936, he married Dalia Menendez Alvarez,
who was about 30 years younger than he.

In 1939 his only son was born:
Francis Wyckoff O'Keefe – Francis O'Keefe, Jr.

He died in 1959 and is buried in Habana, Cuba.

Dalia Menendez Alvarez
Spaniard descent.
Born in 1917, in Habana, Cuba.
Died of Cancer in 1950 or 1951
Wife of Francis O'Keefe.
Mother of Francis Wyckoff O'keefe.

Trip to Cuba:

In January of 1999, I visited Habana from the 9th to the 15th. The reason for the trip was to accompany my mother, for her to see – for the last time – her brothers and to meet all the nieces and nephews born years after our departure from Cuba in 1961. It was an emotional time for all of us who shared this gathering in the old house of El Vedado.

On the 13th, I spent the day verifying information Francis had provided to me about his life in Cuba. I found a former classmate, Félix Lancís Paz, who gave me copies from the school yearbook of St. George, where Francis had attended from Kindergarten through his graduation with a Bachelor of Science in 1957.

Among Félix's memories of Francis, the comment that caught my attention the most was this:

"One thing I remember about Francis is that he was not a coward."
And time will prove him right.

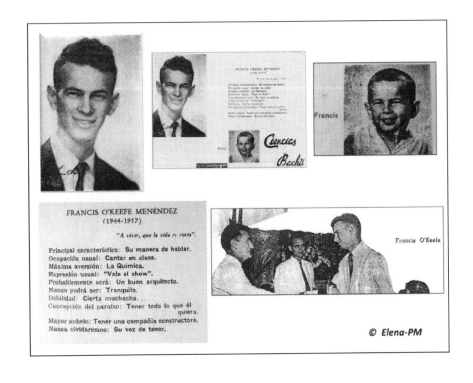

| 2016 Photographed by Mercedes M. Miranda Madruga | Former St. George School Vedado, Habana. | Francis remembered with admiration its architecture and specially the high tower. |

The O'Keefe's apartment building - Habana

Calle Principe #122 – apt. 7 - entre Espada y Hospital – Habana

2016 Google map

That same day I visited the building where Francis had lived until 1961, when he left Cuba for good.

I found the building with an acceptable facade but inside it was all ruined. Francis, his parents and Josefita, at that time his nanny, resided on the top floor. The door to apartment seven was closed. Through the peephole (which was a hole) I put the lens of my camera and I managed to get a good photo of the interior.

I needed all of my courage to go up to apartment seven.
The stairs seemed on the verge of collapse.

On the 2nd floor, I knocked on the door of one of the neighbors. After my introduction and an explanation for my visit, they invited me in to converse. The lady remembered the *americanito* who lived upstairs with his parents and Josefita. I thanked her, said goodbye and gave her $10. In Cuba, visitors nowadays are expected to give a tip even for a greeting. People call dollars *"fulas"* and if you have no *fulas* not even the sun will come out for you.

Cristobal Colon Cemetery, in the city of Habana, dates back to the XIX century.

The next thing was to visit Colon Cemetery to find the graves of his parents. His mother had died of cancer when Francis was about 11 years old. Josefita (Fita) was left to help raise him.

His father died in June 1959. Francis, only 20 years old, was an orphan with no other relatives of relevance in Cuba.

At the offices of Colon, they couldn't find records of Dalia, his mother. On his father, they found the certificate and I obtained a copy after paying a fee. An old, black crippled man, who had been working in the cemetery forever, remembered where the "American" grave was.

When we got there I was disappointed at not being able to read the name, as it looked erased despite having been engraved in marble. The old man crouched and took a stone, and began to rub it against the letters of the name. This to me seemed like a mystical experience when the letters began to appear one by one...

F R A N C I S   O K E E F E

Francis O'Keefe, Sr. - Death Certificate

I returned to Miami. Francis was happy to see me and excited about all the stories, photos and information that I brought for him. He quickly identified the apartment building where he had resided and asked me many questions about my trip.

Francis considered himself Cuban despite being registered at birth as an American citizen, having an Irish name and having lived two-thirds of his life in the United States. Despite an appearance, way of speaking, and behavior very different from the average Cuban, Francis always answered, *"Cuba"* whenever asked where he was from.

Internet Public domain photo.

The years 1939 – 1959

Here are excerpts from the life of Francis, copied from his stories which I recorded on tape and from his papers and floppy disks.

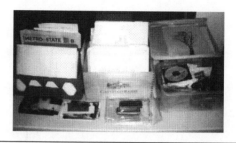

When I was three months old, my parents moved to an apartment in downtown Habana, where I lived until I left Cuba. I only met Manuela Alvarez, my maternal grandmother. My mother was an only child. My father could not stand my mother's cousins, and I just liked Eduardo Alvarez, who gave me his stamps collection.

My father always spoke to me in English and my mother in Spanish. So I grew up bilingual.

My mother enrolled me at the Habana Conservatory.

I was good at "solfeo" music classes, but I couldn't stand the theory, all that about whole notes, half notes, quarter, and eighth notes. Please!

I had two very good dogs: Pete and Fala.

I remember my mother as a young woman, not very tall, thin, black hair, and with a pretty face. My mother died of cancer when I was about 11 years. They took me to my godfather's home. I didn't attend to the funeral.

I accompanied my father on a business trip to Miami when I was about 12 and he bought me a pair of magnificent binoculars. But this Miami was so boring.

My father in Cuba represented American companies in the Construction field. He sold windows, doors, furnaces, steel structures, and several other materials.

We were not rich but we lived well. Once he gave me a Rolleiflex camera, one of the best at that time, which he bought for his business but later gave it to me.

I learned to dance to Cuban music when I was 12 with the nieces of the maid Josefita. They were about my age. One of them was a very good dancer.

The only sport I think I was good at was Squash. Also, I was a fast runner.

I was 15 when I came to visit my aunt Georgia at her home in Abiquiu, New Mexico. It was a small town. I spent 3 months there. During my stay a couple came from New York to visit Georgia. And my aunt said to me, "I do not know what to do, this couple traveled together from NY, so I'm putting them in the same room." My aunt was grumpy. Instead of dessert she would serve salad, can you imagine?

In 1957 I graduated with a Bachelor in Science from St. George School. That year there was no prom and we all went to celebrate at Tropicana.

In 1958 I started studying architecture at the *Universidad de Villanueva*, it was there I got to understand Calculus. Calculus is a sum - there are mathematical formulas for calculating volumes and irregular areas - like how to calculate the flow of a lake. In Geometry I had no problem it was very easy for me. At Villanueva I only studied for a few months and then I transferred to the Universidad de La Habana, which for political affairs had disturbances and it was even closed for a while.

My father and I talked just a few times during our lives, except for the last year that we went out for walks perhaps, because he already foresaw his death. On June 1, 1959 my father died in a clinic of a heart attack.

I stayed in the same household with Josefita. I also tried to keep my father's business going and to continue with my studies. It was then that I wrote to my aunt Georgia for help.

As we all know, on January 1st, 1959 Fidel Castro took power in Cuba, and from that day on everything began to change in the country; and not precisely for the better.

Correspondence with Georgia

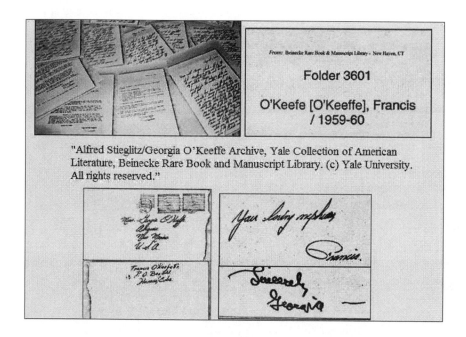

Orphaned at the age of 20, and residing in a country that for the first time made him an outsider under the slogans of "Yankee Go Home", it was under these circumstances that Francis O'Keefe, Jr. was forced to make decisions about how to continue on with his life. Among the first things he did was to contact his now famous and rich aunt Georgia.

My interpretation of this correspondence (June 1959 - July 1960) between Georgia and Francis is that there was a a lack of understanding between them regarding the kind of life in Cuba versus the one in USA. Georgia had never visited Cuba and was unaware of the lifestyle on the island. Francis, for his part, was better informed about the American culture. But equally, neither one could predict what was coming at the political level.

With the Revolution of 1959, relations between Cuba and the U.S. were to deteriorate gradually as history has confirmed.

Francis asked Georgia for some financial assistance mainly to continue his studies of Architecture in Habana and to meet his basic needs which were about $100 per month. Francis worked during the daytime in the same line of business his father worked, and he attended the university at night.

Georgia promised to send $ 100.00 monthly and she did.

Francis loved Cuba and felt that there, upon graduation; he would have a great future. But things got complicated because of the political system that was being established. Eventually, he understood that he couldn't live in Cuba any longer and began discussing with Georgia about moving to the States.

In January of 1960, Francis wanted to leave the country and to come to study at some of the universities in USA. Georgia suggested other universities, etc. Francis also mentioned a girlfriend whom he was considering for marriage and talked about Fita (*the lady who lives with me and attends to the house*). He wanted for the three of them to leave Cuba together.

(2006 06-0150 -Unknown photographer. Francis O'Keefe and Unidentified Woman, 1960 - Gelatin silver print. Gift of the Georgia O'Keeffe Foundation - Georgia O'Keeffe Museum)

Some of their letters are amusing because of their different ways of thinking and cultural backgrounds.

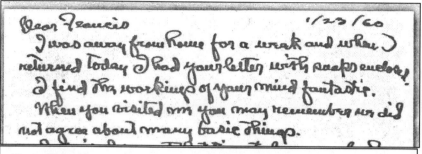

Dear Francis
I was away from home for a week and when I returned today
I had yout letter with snaps enclosed.
I find the workings of your mind fantastic.
When you visited me you may remember we did not agree about
many basic things.

Dear Francis:
I have read your letter again today and I think I must
write you again. You seem to have so little sense.
If you think you must leave Cuba you must plan to leave
alone. Don't think you can take care of three people here
till you have proved that you can take care of one.

Excerpt from letter dated Feb. 23, 1960

I wish you would write me about the
woman who has always cared for you.
Send me a picture of her if you can.
Is she in good health and how old is she?
Let me hear from you   Sincerely
Georgia

Francis's reply dated March 14,1960

What about Fita? She started with my parents 2 years
before I was born. And, she stopped earning anything a long time ago.
She is colored, 52 years old, strong, hard worker, and can take good care
of a house. I am sure I will need her in Alburquerque. Besides I can't
leave her alone. I owe a great deal to her.

Based on Francis letter from April 11,1960 it seems Georgia dis-
aproved of Fita.

April 11, 1960.

Dear aunt Georgia,

I am quite surprised to hear that you do not want
Fita! She has been like a second mother to me. I told you in another
letter that I was not going to leave her.

Dear aunt Georgia,
          I am quite surprise to hear that you do not want
Fita! She has been like a second mother to me. I told you in another
letter that I was not going to leave her.

Exchange of projects, suggestions and concepts between them went on for several months. Francis proposed a plan and Georgia refuted, sometimes rightly and sometimes not understanding Francis's points of view or the situation in which he was.

However she did help him financially. Francis was also a bit of a dreamer while Georgia was more realistic. The issue was that they couldn't come to an agreement most of the time.

Finally, in 1961 Francis left Cuba by himself. The relationship with the girlfriend had ended and Fita came a few years later to live permanently in the U.S.

Francis arrived from Habana to Miami, Florida in January of 1961. He traveled in the second plane that left Cuba after the breakdown of relations between the two countries.

-On January 3, 1961 the US withdrew diplomatic recognition of the Cuban government and closed the embassy in Havana. – Internet: Wikipedia and History.com

Once at the airport in Miami, Francis phoned some friends and former associates of his father (Francis O'Keefe, Sr.), who came to pick him up and take him to dinner. Then he was offered work as a draftsman in their office (I never knew their names, only that they were Americans) and they let him stay and live in an empty room in the offices located in Key Biscayne. After a month, they informed him that they could not continue helping him.

1960's Miami - City Data.

Brigade 2506 – CIA

-In 1960 President Eisenhower quietly authorized the Central Intelligence Agency (CIA) to organize, train, and equip Cuban refugees as a guerrilla force to overthrow Castro. - www.globalsecurity.org.

Francis had had prior contact with the MRP group (People's Revolutionary Movement) which was founded in May of 1960. This organization offered him work in their offices but Francis instead chose to go to military training camps. There he was until the group was transferred to Guatemala, based in the mountains near a town called Retalhuleo, where they remained for approximately one month. They were returned to Miami after having confirmed the failure of the invasion.

On April 17, 1961, 1400 Cuban exiles launched what became a botched invasion at the Bay of Pigs on the southern coast of Cuba .- http://www.jfklibrary.org/JFK/JFK-in-History/The-Bay-of-Pigs.

C.I.A. #	BRIGADA #	NOMBRE	
2323	4188	FRANCIS O'KEEFE MENENDEZ	BON7

BATALLON 7 INFANTERIA - MANUEL MARTINEZ ARBONA, Jefe BON.

Notice that the C.I.A. used Francis's maternal surname, Menendez, to make him appear officially as Cuban, even though he was registered at birth at the U.S. Embassy in Cuba as Francis Wyckoff O'Keefe.

Back in Miami, the C.I.A assigned a salary to each participant of the 2506 Brigade.

Francis received $240 monthly for 6 months. He rented a room in a family house and bought a car - Henry J.

I had never before heard mention of this brand of car. *Wikipedia: Henry J was produced and sold from 1950 -1954.*

Francis wrote to his aunts: To Aunt Ida, with whom he had exchanged correspondence since childhood, who lived in a small town called Whittier in California. To Aunt Claudia, who lived in Beverly Hills, also in California. And Georgia also wrote to him.

He spoke by phone with Claudia, who informed him that Ida was in a coma in a Los Angeles hospital. She invited him to go to California with her. Francis accepted the invitation. Claudia and his cousin, June, of whose existence he had been unaware, went to pick him up at the airport.

He arrived in time to see his aunt Ida, who died shortly after.

He then went to reside with Claudia in her home at 221 S. Camden Drive, Beverly Hills. Aunt Claudia bought him a Fiat 500 with a sun roof.

(RC-1999-001-157 Unknown photographer
Georgia O'Keeffe and Claudia O'Keeffe, 1972
Color photograph Claudia O'Keeffe Papers, Georgia O'Keeffe Museum)

In the summer of 2013, I visited the Brigade 2506 Museum located in Miami. There I was greeted kindly by Mr. Vicente Blanco-Capote, one of the first to join the list of brigadiers in 1960. After showing him proofs of Francis's identity he accepted his photo. It would be placed with the rest of the brigadiers' photos, hung on the walls of the museum.

The Bay of Pigs Museum, also known as the Brigade 2506 Museum.

1960's U.S.NAVY

The Vietnam War - 1959 - 1975

1961 -President John F. Kennedy orders more help for the South Vietnamese government in its war against the Vietcong guerrillas. – Battlefield:Vietnam- PBS.org.

On September 25, 1961 Francis enlisted in the U.S. Armed Forces. In those years military service was compulsory. If a man of military age was willing to volunteer instead of waiting to be called, he would be allowed to choose which branch of the Armed Forces to serve.

Francis, wanting to continue his architectural studies, chose to serve with the "Construction Battalion."

> *A common initialism for "Construction Battalion" CB, which is similar phonetically to the words, "Sea Bee," gave birth to one of the emblems of the branches of the United States Navy. - Official site on the internet: http://www.seabee.navy.mil/*

While waiting to be called for Service, Francis obtained employment with a company that produced manuals for the mechanics of the 707 passenger aircraft. He worked for a year for this company.
In April of 1963 he was called to active duty with the U.S. Navy to serve with the Seabees.

He was trained at the Naval Construction Battalion Center in Port Hueneme, on America's west coast.

After the training he sailed to the seas of Asia. He spent three months at sea, and then he went to Yokosuka Base in Japan.

In the Vietnam War, U.S. military bases in Japan, especially in Okinawa, were used as important strategic and logistical points. – Wikipedia

On his days off, Francis used his time to learn Japanese and to visit some points of interest, including the hot springs of Hakone.

> Japanese by Francis:
> KATAKANA – 46 basic characters for foreign words.
> HIRAGANA – 46 basic characters to write Japanese words.
> KANJI – Characters originally from China.

On August 2, 1964, the U.S. destroyer Maddox exchanged shots with North Vietnamese torpedo boats in the Gulf of Tonkin. - http://www.history.com/news/the-gulf-of-tonkin-incident

After this incident, the company in which Francis was allocated was transported to Vietnam waters, where they remained for 45 days on combat alert.

In 1965 he completed his term of military service. One of the officers offered him an opportunity to join the OCS (Officer Candidate School.) Francis rejected this proposal due to his obsession with completing his degree in Architecture.

"Example/Photo of the
Medal of Expeditionary."

Francis was discharged honorably and was awarded the "Medal of Expeditionary" for having stayed those 45 days in a combat zone.

Seaman (SN, E3): E3 paygrades, Seaman (SN), Hospitalman (HN), Airman (AN), Fireman (FN) and *Constructionman (CN)* are the highest non-rated ranks in the Navy.
www.pbs.org/weta/carrier/naval_ranks

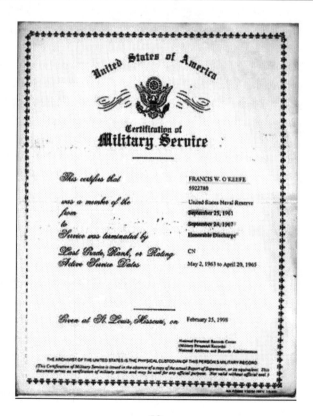

1965-1972 University

Upon completion of the military service in 1965, Francis returned to live at Claudia's residence. Then he went to work for a construction company. After a while he rented his own apartment. By then he had given up on finishing Architecture since the only university that offered this career was USC (University of Southern California) and it was unaffordable.

In 1966 or '67 Francis arranged for Josefita ('Fita) to travel from Cuba to the U.S. She went to live at Claudia's in the capacity of a domestic employee.

In 1968 Francis began to study at San Fernando Valley State College (now known as California State University at Northridge, or CSUN). In June of 1970 he obtained a Bachelor of Arts in Political Science. After that he registered at the University of California.

Francis: "My contact with a psychologist was to write my master paper for the Master of Arts at UCLA: "Analytical Psychology and Revolution: a Proposal for the Transposition of Psychotherapeutic methods to the Collectivity."

He graduated on June 13, 1972 with a Masters in Latin American Studies. He worked for a time at UCLA as a research assistant.

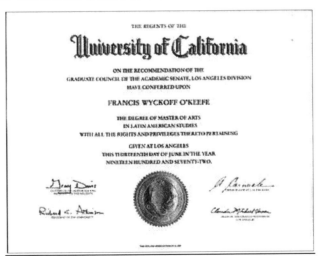

We acquired this copy of the diploma in March, 2000, at a cost of $60.00 Francis was proudly happy to receive it.

Difficult Years

In the mid-1970s Francis began hearing voices (mainly Fita's) which made him feel ill and disoriented. Nonetheless, he continued working as a draftsman for an engineering company until 1974. Apparently (as per his Social Security records) he worked odd jobs between 1975 and 1981.

From 1975 on, Fita began to help him financially. He barely understood the new psychosomatic health issue that he was suffering. He rented a small apartment at Hauser Blvd. & 8th Street in Los Angeles, where the refrigerator was almost always empty. He had no friends, he could not work and he even forgot that he had a university degree.

▼ **Make sure we have recorded every year you worked.**

(If you live outside the U.S., follow the directions at the bottom of page 4.)

Your Earnings Record at a Glance

Years You Worked	Your Taxed Social Security Earnings	Your Taxed Medicare Earnings	Years You Worked	Your Taxed Social Security Earnings	Your Taxed Medicare Earnings
1960	$ 381		1980	$ 123	$ 123
1961	1,271		1981	720	720
1962	3,229		1982	0	0
1963	905	Medicare	1983	0	0
1964	1,787	Began in 1966	1984	0	0
1965	2,507		1985	0	0
1966	5,760	$ 5,760	1986	0	0
1967	2,033	2,033	1987	0	0
1968	0	0	1988	0	0
1969	1,027	1,027	1989	0	0
1970	2,480	2,480	1990	0	0
1971	466	466	1991	0	0
1972	3,310	3,310	1992	0	0
1973	8,349	8,349	1993	0	0
1974	5,847	5,847	1994	0	0
1975	50	50	1995	0	0
1976	778	778	1996	0	0
1977	0	0	1997	0	0
1978	0	0	1998	0	0
1979	0	0	1999	Not yet recorded	

Totals over your working career:

Estimated taxes paid for Social Security:
You paid: $1,753
Your employers paid: $1,689

Estimated taxes paid for Medicare:
You paid: $223
Your employers paid: $217

Note: **If you are self-employed, you pay the total tax on your net earnings.**

———3———

In 1980 he traveled to Miami on an airplane, in search of employment. He found no job. From there he took off on foot and hitchhiked all the way back to Los Angeles. Once in L.A. he went to live on the streets.

Josefita died in 1982; Aunt Claudia in 1984.

(2006-06-0809 Unknown photographer
Georgia O'Keeffe with Josefita Pino (Fita), c. 1980s
Color photograph Gift of the Georgia O'Keeffe Foundation Georgia O'Keeffe Museum)

Francis:

"Claudia left me in her will the sum of $100 to be received monthly for life. There was a fight over her will that involved Lucas Kamel or Lucas Carmel (Claudia's administrator). I did not participate and the checks stopped. The last check I received was in December, 1985."

Lonely Traveler

1985-1987 Traveling through North Mexico:

Francis left Los Angeles and crossed the U.S.-Mexico border via Baja California. Arriving in Rosarito Beach, a city that belongs to the metropolitan area of Tijuana, he sought shelter in a church. A priest took him in and got him a job in a school. After a while he continued his journey to Juarez, where he met a Cuban-Mexican who gave him a job as a watchman, allowed him to sleep in the garage and gave him some money for food.

The next stop was Piedras Negras, where someone gave him a bicycle. He then rode to Brownsville where he spent several months. At a cafe where he went to ask for something to eat, he was served by the lady-owner of the place, who after speaking with him and understanding his situation, offered to pay one month's stay in a hotel nearby. Days later he traveled to Matamoros (26 miles from Brownsville) and found employment at the newspaper, "El Bravo de Matamoros," as a translator of English writings into Spanish.

Francis: "Mexico is very friendly and even the police were always very attentive."

In mid-1987 Francis decided to return to the U.S. In Brownsville, on the American side, he was questioned on suspicion of smuggling Mexicans. He had no documents; he had lost his wallet on a bus. Only after the agents were satisfied with the questioning was he allowed to enter American territory.

1987 - Traveling USA South heading for Florida:

Francis was given several used bikes along his way, and when they broke down he left them on the side of the road. Hitchhiking, riding a bike and walking, he went from town to town. In some of these towns he went to police stations, asking for shelter. Most of the time he was allowed to sleep in a cell and in the morning they offered him coffee. Eventually, he arrived in the city of New Orleans, where he was lodged in the Bishop's house.

He stayed for a few weeks during which he worked in the Bishop's garden. Up to this point he had traveled about 2,000 miles.

Florida! Here is one of many papers written by Francis, fortunately this one was typed. So, I'm copying and pasting:

Subject: Arrest in Jacksonville

I went to Jacksonville. Went to a church and obtained employ for a short while. I had left my things, a bag full of papers I had written, too heavy to carry, under a table outside a Jiffy Lube station.

I returned to it and found them gone. At night I was near, at a gasoline station, where I asked for a cup of coffee. Three adolescents came over and began to speak, and mentioned Jiffy Lube, an incident that was strange. I walked away, saw a policeman, told him the story and he dismissed it. I sat on a bench. After a few minutes the same policeman came and arrested me, taking me to a house where several police cars were. I was identified as being not the one sought, but instead of being released I was taken to the police station to be photographed and finger-printed. The woman at the station was nervous, and said that the machine for taking fingerprints was broken. The policeman nevertheless took a photograph of me. On the way out, in the car, he read to me the "Miranda Rights".

Angry, I hitchhiked to Tallahassee to file a complaint at the Office of the Governor. There, I spoke to a woman about the matter, another sitting at a desk, and a policeman entered, called by them, to whom she pretended to complain about my wild behavior there. I had been calm and remained calm. She lied; why?

Outside a police car awaited me with the emergency lights on, the policeman on the passenger's side waving goodbye to me. One block away another policeman, one on duty at a building, stopped me and told me he did not want me around there.

Francis kept going south along the East Coast. He stayed for a short time in several cities until he reached Fort Lauderdale and there he found an office building at U.S. 1 and 45th St. where he was able to sleep at night. Some people helped him with food and money, and one man gave him a sleeping bag; this last item is the most valuable thing that a homeless person can receive.

Not far from this location was Imperial Point Library, a place to read, to write, to draw and to take a nap.

In December of 1993, Francis had a minor car accident – he was a pedestrian. Case #93-190352 documents the incident: Paramedics arrived and took him to a nearby hospital where he stayed for two days.

"Incident with police in Fort Lauderdale.

In 1994, after the accident, I still unable to walk well, I crossed US1 and had to remain in the median because the time allotted for pedestrians to cross at that corner, the same where I had been hit by a car, was only of seven seconds. A police automobile was stopped, after crossing 45th Street, in the fast lane, going towards the South, and a big, and very fat, police officer came out and ordered me to cross the street!, in a very threatening manner."

A few days later he headed to Miami-Dade.

"Having just arrived in Miami, while sleeping on a bench I was arrested and taken to a Police Station. I was told to wait in a room, after a while I learned that I could leave. Just like that, without a cause or an excuse."

He wandered through Hialeah, Miami Springs and Coral Gables till he found an area that pleased him. It was at Florida International University. Here Francis found a friendly atmosphere. He was even allowed to use FIU - 1557 SW 107th Ave., Miami, FL 33174 as his mailing address, and in one of the offices they kept a box with all of Francis's many written papers, safe for him till the autumn of 1999 when I accompanied him to pick it up.

PLEASE REPLY TO: FACSIMILE (305) 374-4406
Fort Lauderdale
Direct Line: (305) 847-3399

May 9, 1995

Mr. Francis O'Keefe
1557 S.W. 107th Avenue
Miami, FL 33174

At the offices of Children and Families he was approved to receive money per month in Food Stamps.

One day Francis found West Dade Regional library and the park surrounding it and made it his favorite spot. Several good people, who talked to him and noticed his mental condition as well as his elegant and cultivated personality, helped him from time to time with a backpack, a jacket or money.

A lady gave him a nice bicycle (La Niña) on which he went everywhere in the city. By then Francis was 57 years old.

About a year and a half later we were going to meet.

Souto v. O'Keefe

1999 February

After I met Francis and learned about his mental health condition I began to look for an agency or an organization that could help him. I didn't know then what a bureaucratic and hypocritical "welfare system" we have in Miami.

Someone suggested that I ask Commissioner Souto, who used the library once a month for his Town Meetings. The day came and I went to him as he was sitting in a chair reading a newspaper.

I: "Mr. Souto?"

Souto: "Yes?" He was seated and looked at me with an expression like, "What do you want?"

I said, "Excuse me," and I sat in front of him. "See, I want to know if you could help me to help this gentleman who is homeless and..." I explained the case to him in the simplest way possible.

Souto: "Yes," (contemptuously) "I know who he is, he wants no help."

By now, I had taken notice of Souto's lack of manners and arrogant attitude. I asked him, "Well, could you tell me where to go to see if I can work something out for him?"

From the inside of the left pocket of his jacket he withdrew a book and gave me two phone numbers.

I said, "Thank you." I do not think he answered.

The next day from home I called the two phone numbers. One belonged to a residence and they had no idea what I was asking. The other number was disconnected.

A few days later I was called to the office of the library manager, Cathie Conduite, who gave me a memo in which I was scolded for having dared to consult the commissioner about a personal matter. Apparently wanting to help a homeless man was not a social problem, but a personal matter - like selling Avon products.

By the way, Ms. Conduite was a very fine library manager. I'm certain she was forced to act in a *politically correct* manner because of Souto's complaint.

"The infinitely small have a pride infinitely great." — Voltaire

2010 - Sept. on TV channel 41

The Pandora Box

Opening Pandora's box was what I accomplished by addressing the Commissioner. A few days later began the harassing of Francis in particular, and on two other homeless men who never bothered anyone and were regulars at the WDR library.

In Pottinger v. Miami, a Federal Court held that punishing people for sleeping in public when they had no alternative place to sleep violated their right to be free from cruel and unusual punishment under the Eighth Amendment and violated their right to travel. As a result, homeless people in Miami cannot be arrested for sleeping in public places if they have no alternative.
-Copyright 1999 Kristen Brown is a legal advocate at The National Law Center on Homelessness and Poverty,

In Michael Pottinger, Peter Carter, Berry Young, et al. v. City of Miami (810 F. Supp. 1551 [1992]), the U.S. District Court for the Southern District of Florida ruled that the city's practices were "cruel and unusual," in violation of the Eighth Amendment's ban against punishment based on status. (Only the homeless were being arrested.) Furthermore, the court found the police practices of taking or destroying the property of the homeless to be in violation of Fourth and Fifth Amendment rights of freedom from unreasonable seizure and confiscation of property.

However, it is one thing what a Federal Court decides, and it is something else what some politicians and some members of the Police Department of Miami think and do.

Monday, February 8, 1999 2:12 PM
From: "Francis O'Keefe" <ovejas9@yahoo.com>
To: EPM15@yahoo.com
Elena,
Anado, the sergeant threatened to arrest me if he saw me again in the library, as well as Dade County, leaving unclear whether both, but in reference to the Libraries he will arrest me for "trespassing after-warning" if I returned

---

Tuesday, February 9, 1999 5:57 PM
From<epm15@yahoo.com>View
To: "FRANCIS W. O'KEEFE" OVEJAS9@YAHOO.COM

Francis,

I just took the liberty to go to your "apartment" and picked up 2 bags, with the things I find most important, we do not know if they're going to be here stealing or throwing away. I put the bags in my car. Take care. Write to me. Always, Elena

----

Wednesday, February 10, 1999 11:48 AM
From:"Elena" epm15@yahoo.com
To:"Francis O'Keefe" " ovejas9@yahoo.com

Francis, Last night I spoke to my friend the Policeman, and he explained that there is an order: Do not allow anyone to sleep in the park after closing time. For the rest everything remains the same.

Around here the Gordo and the other gentleman who has the shopping cart still around. This Policeman, checked the computer and said that there is no arrest warrant for you. I need to inform you that on Friday the weather is going to change, rain and low temperatures. I work until Friday at 6pm.

If you come back you can go to my house for the weekend. By Monday, we can find another park or somewhere near the library where you can camp. Or perhaps you will prefer a site in Miami Springs, there is a library there and you'll be close to the bicycle shop. And how is "la Niña? Is she behaving? I await your response.
Hugs, Elena

Francis returned that Friday, February 12, which happened to be his birthday. I brought them both (Francis and his bike) to my house, where I lived alone with two dogs. I gave him the guest room. Francis took a shower and I gave him the clean clothes that I had saved for him. Then we sat at the table, ate, talked, and in celebration of his 60th birthday I opened a bottle of apple cider. I didn't dare offer him any alcoholic beverages, I felt 99% calm but there was this 1% reminding me that Francis was schizophrenic.

After the 10 pm newscasts before going to sleep I warned him: "Francis, I live alone and I have a 38 revolver. I have engraved in my mind that, if one night I wake up and see someone in my room, I will take the 38 I keep under the pillow and I will shoot. Then I'll see who got killed and next I'll call 911. I say this because if you need anything do not go in my room! Knock on the door and call me."

Francis paid real close attention to my words. I left him in the living room watching television and in the morning I found him sleeping in one of the sofas. We had breakfast and went to the library. There, we took some pictures with Enrique who was his friend. That evening we returned to my house.

Francis liked my house, but much more he liked my dogs Allura and Apolo; they sensed Francis's good nature and always followed him and lay down beside him.

Yellow Car & Home

1999 - Feb. 12 - 60 years old

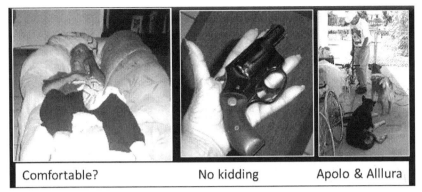

Comfortable?　　　　　No kidding　　　　Apolo & Alllura

We had a good time during those few days. However, I don't know exactly why, but I could not keep Francis at my home for good. He understood. On Monday, he was back at West Dade.

Enrique Stratchan

When Francis saw our picture he laughingly commented,
"We look like an American couple of retirees living in Costa Rica."

<u>Bureau-cracy</u>

Much "blah, blah, blah," but zero results. During the months of February and March of 1999, representatives of the DHS visited the library. Through them I got the names and phone numbers of other agencies that could help resolve the situation of Francis. These were the responses:

"We do not handle this type of case."

"Please contact this other agency."

"We cannot give you any information, the applicant must call."

"We cannot take your call now, leave your name and phone number ."

Beep!

FROM: ALPHONSO ARGUELLO
TO: epm15@yahoo.com
<u>Tuesday, February 23, 1999 8:22 PM</u>
> elena for francis to get an apartment he must have an
income, food stamp is not a financial input source.
If he has none, then the only option will be to go to a shelter and
once he gets a job they will assist him in finding him an apartment.

One afternoon I was outside the library when I saw Souto arriving and going straight to where Francis kept his things in plastic boxes. I informed Francis, so we collected the most important things and put them in my car. And .... Bingo! Three days later all the remaining stuff was gone. I mentioned it to the social worker and he said it had been ordered by Souto.

As nothing was resolved by any of the social assistance agencies with regard to Francis, I continued taking care of him according to my abilities. On one occasion I took him to Community Health of South Dade (CHI), where he was seen by a general practitioner.

Some weekends I would invite him to my house, and also allowed him to use my home as his mailing address.

Francis continued his normal life, but changed his location to sleep at night.

"And where do you sleep now? " I asked.

"Under Souto's offices."

"Whaaaat?"

"Yes, I am well protected there because, there is a security guard on duty, and at 6 a.m., before leaving, he wakes me up."

Ha, ha! Like "sleeping with the enemy."

Where is O'Keefe?

In the last days of July of 1999, Francis's bike was tied up to the front of the library but inside there was no sign of Francis. I was surprised not to see him throughout the day, especially with the bike out there. When I got home I started calling the hospitals asking for "O'Keefe" and/or "John Doe." Fortunately he was not at any of them. The weekend went by and nothing. Nada!

I talked to Manny Gomez, a police officer friend of my family, who first tried to dissuade me of my search. When I insisted he said, "He might have been arrested."

On Monday, August 2, after work and before getting home, I stopped by the South Dade Police Station, where I found that Francis had been arrested on July 29. I was given the following information:

Prisoner # 9963954; TGKDC /Stockade Prison – Tel. 305-470-7600.

When I called I was informed that the next day (August 3) Francis was going for a hearing at the courthouse in the Civic Center: Case # M-99-41049. Francis would be in courtroom 6-7. The next morning at 9 a.m. I was in the courthouse. A young Hispanic bailiff, who would not let me enter the courtroom, assured me that Francis was going to be acquitted. Why this wretched bailiff lied to me, I do not know. After waiting for over an hour, I found that room 6-7 was empty. The prisoners had left through another inside door.

Someone informed me that they would have taken Francis to Dade County Jail before being transported back to TGK. So, there I went. My sole interest was to let Francis know that I was aware of his situation.

Upon my arrival I found myself facing a window where the officers knew less of the process than I. Finally I learned that Francis had just been bused back to TGK/Stockade. Cell S-4.

In the evening I spoke with an officer on duty at TGK. I wanted to know when I could visit Francis, if I could call him on a phone, who was his lawyer, and so on. In the past 24 hours I had spoken with half of the officers who work the phones at that site. I learned that the type of jail where they kept Francis was only for misdemeanor cases, such as drunk drivers, drug addicts, or someone for giving a slap to an impertinent photographer. This gave me great peace of mind; I had imagined Francis among a mob of criminals of the first order.

That same night of August 3rd, TGK told me that every detainee had a specific day and visiting hours assigned. O'Keefe's day was Thursday. What they did not explain to me was that for a prisoner to receive visits he needed to put the name of the visitor on a list. Francis, of course, didn't know this and had not been able to get my phone number.

On Thursday, August 5th I went to visit, for the first time in my life, a jail and a prisoner. I went through a hallway swarmed with spikes. At the end was an office with a double-glazed window, two benches for visitors, and a wall with three rows of lockers without locks. What were they for? I wondered.

It turned out that their purpose was to keep everything that a visitor could carry: wallet, glasses, car keys, umbrella, etc... Everything except the clothes one was wearing. I returned to my car and left my purse in the trunk. My keys I had no choice but to leave them in the locker without a lock.

Visitors are prohibited from wearing:

- Clothing that resembles a correctional employee.
- Clothing that resembles an inmate uniform.
- Hats or head covering.
- Tight-fitting, see-through, provocative clothing of any kind, e.g. athletic shorts, hot pants.
- Tops that are low-cut; revealing more than two inches of cleavage, strapless shirts.
- Skirts and dresses more than 2 inches above the knee, e.g.,
- micro/miniskirts.
- Non-prescription sunglasses.
- Hooded garments.
- Clothing with offensive lettering.

It was also forbidden to kiss a prisoner on the mouth. Really, that type of kiss was not on my agenda.

I went to the window to register and was informed that I was not on the list ... Oh, no! What list?

The officer to whom I had presented my driver's license and Dade County Employee ID agreed to make an exception because I was a county employee and proceeded to call O'Keefe to ask if he wanted to accept my visit.

When the time came all visitors went down a long hallway and through security checks. In a large room with long benches right and left - like a chapel - we sat down to await the arrival of prisoners.

They all – except Francis - arrived in line. Five minutes went by and there I was sitting alone without my prisoner.

Finally, Francis came in. He was dressed in creamy overalls,was very clean, shaved, and had gained a few pounds. He had a cheerful expression on his face. We hugged and sat down to talk. He said the prison routine was acceptable and there were no conflicts of any kind.

I handed him the notes that library staff had written for him. He explained how it worked for receiving or making phone calls, and other matters related to his stay in TGK.

Visiting time ended and we parted, both of us more relieved; I for having found Francis, and Francis for having been found by me.
For sure, we complemented each other very well.

Turner Guilford Knight Correctional Center, also known as TGK, is the principal detention center to process people arrested in Miami-Dade County, Florida

Visiting Day

On July 29, 1999, Miami-Dade residents voted on whether to adopt a penny tax to fund public transportation. Proponents of the measure paid O'Keefe $75 to stand outside Coral Park Senior High to distribute flyers in favor of the proposal.

NARRATIVE CONTINUATION

MIAMI-DADE POLICE DEPARTMENT

According to V#1, he and W#1 arrived at Coral Park Senior High to vote. V#1 stepped out of W#1's vehicle and went to photograph A#1 who was in front of the school wearing a T-shirt "VOTE #70" and handing out pamphlets to vote yes on the elections. A#1 not wanting to be photographed, swung with a closed fist striking the camera which subsequently struck V#1 in the eye. V#1 backed off and A#1 was detained by W#2 school security until our arrival. School Board Officer J. Diaz was also on scene, but didn't witness the battery. W#1 stated that he saw A#1 punch V#1 for no apparent reason. A#1 stated that he went to shield the camera from taking his picture when he "touched" V#1 on the shoulder. V#1 stated his eye bothered him but no injury was observed.

A#1 taken to T.G.K.

D3300 Sgt. Giebler responded to scene.

Account of the Incident by Francis:

==

"On the 29th of July of 1999 I went to give out pamphlets in favor of the proposal of the 1 cent tax increase, during the elections at Coral Park Senior High. At noon, the students came out. I took a seat I had been offered by a neighbor and sat away from the main door, waiting for the students to leave.

At 5:10 in the afternoon a small, old, red car arrived. I went to hand out a pamphlet to the passenger. He looked at me, his mouth puckered and smiling in a gesture of mockery, holding a camera in his hands. I tried to hand to him a pamphlet but could not for he would not make a move to take it, and he continued to mock me. He stepped out of the car, stepped back one step, and aimed the camera at me still mocking me in the same way. I lifted my hand in front of the camera, extending my arm, blocking the photographing, and said to him, politely, "Do not photograph me, please." , and he then moved to my left, in little jumps, he slightly obese, his body soft, of about forty years of age, so as to photograph me from another angle.

I thought there was nothing else I could do but, and slapped the camera away. In doing so I almost fell, needing to support myself by touching him under his left shoulder, he also almost falling. He was scared, I seeing it as we were almost falling.

Then I heard a voice behind me say "Assault and battery, I saw it!", "Assault and battery, I saw it!", which after I looked, and saw a slim, old man, he kept repeating "Assault and battery, I saw it!".

I then felt threated by both of them, and I went to the police automobile of the school parked on the grass a few meters from us. The two school police officers stepped out of the car.

The man (Bernardo Escobar)with the camera walked by and looking at me and pointing at me with his arm outstretched and index finger straight towards me asked me "Are you not the one [at the library]?", to which I answered yes with a nod of my head. He had seen me there. But why the insinuation that that was something bad, as he indicated?

The first officer separated me from the two that arrived in the red car, while the old man, who was said to be elected as Commissioner of the 10th District of Miami-Dade County Javier Souto, began to photograph me and to exclaim: "So you don't want to be photographed!", and took a photograph, taking immediately afterwards several photographs as he repeated this before taking each photograph like a maniac.

Souto could photograph me at his will, the officers there not stopping him, he obviously in defiance of them, exclaiming what he exclaimed, and so to provoke me further. I stood reclining my arm over a pole, while the school police remained there and Souto kept photographing.

Miami-Dade Metro Police arrived. They questioned me, and they questioned them, and that it had been said that I had hit with my fist the man, as well as only the camera, and the camera then hitting the face of the man.

Yet later I read the report: stated that I had hit the camera, and that the camera hit the man holding it.

Who said I hit the man directly?

One of the Metro-Miami-Dade officers asked me to take the contents out of my pockets, and handcuffed and placed me inside the automobile of the police. Inside the police car I felt claustrophobic, a terrible sensation acquired from so many unjust arrests.

I told the policeman sitting on the passenger's side and he turned on the air-conditioning, which caused a slight betterment of the situation. I was taken to Stockade prison.

They know it is illegal to do what they did, and yet did it, and this is not because they are not intelligent, but because they are thugs.

==

I can imagine how scared Escobar might have been when Francis, who was about 20 years older, a bit shorter and weighted about 40 pounds less than Escobar, dared to throw a slap at his camera.
LOL!

I have asked myself, what happened with the photos Souto took of Francis? Did he make an album? What a sick obsession this guy had with O'Keefe!

> *"Weak men cannot handle power.*
> *It will either crush them,*
> *or they will use it to crush others"*
> — *Jocelyn Murray*

Court Hearing - Trial

Miami Dade County is the 11th judicial circuit of Florida, the largest and busiest of Florida's 20 judicial circuits. Each circuit has its own elected public defender responsible for representing people who face the loss of their liberty and are determined by the court to be unable to pay for a private attorney. - Internet

After my first visit to Francis at TGK I tried to get in touch with his public defenders. Their names were Garrett Zediker and Robert Goldman. I don't remember if they returned my calls. I wanted them to change the plea of *nolo contendere* to that of not guilty.

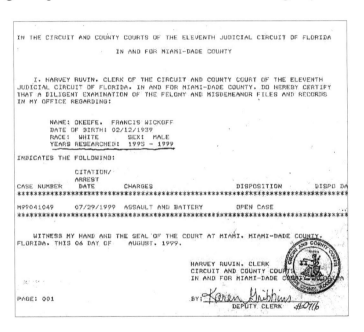

Francis and I spoke on the phone every day for about an hour.

The following Thursday, August 12, I went back to TGK to drop some clothes for 'Judgment Day.'

The Day of the Trial – August 17 - I was able to speak with attorney Goldman for five minutes. I wanted him to defend Francis and plead not guilty, but he said, *"He does not have a chance because he is a homeless and there is a politician involved."*

Since then every time I hear the mystic "Liberty and Justice for all" I just have to laugh.

Summary as written by Francis :

===

FIRST APPEARANCE: This happened the morning after my arrest, July 30, when I was taken into a large room, to face a judge on a large TV screen. I was informed of the date (Aug. 3) for my next appearance in court (Arraignment or Pre-Trial, who knows?)
Also, I was offered a Public Defender. Then, I was in a claustrophobic bus to TGK.

On Aug. 3rd, I appeared before Judge Steve Leifman. At this court there were two attorneys – Mr. Zediket and Mr. Goldman. They didn't discuss my case with me nor any of the procedures were explained to me as it is stipulated by the Law.
The Judge was a low talker, so most of us (the accusers) couldn't understand a word he said. My trial was set for the August 17.
Then I was taken to a social worker who told me that I could be set free if I had a telephone number where I could be reached, which I didn't have and couldn't remember Elena's phone number.
All this time Elena was outside the courtroom pleading with a Hispanic bailiff to inform me that she was there and he kept telling her "don't worry he is going to be freed in a short while, just wait out here."
She did wait till past noon time until there was no one left.
That was it for me that day; back to TGK.
Nonetheless, on Aug. 5, she came to visit me. For the first time since my arrest I felt protected.

A few days later I was taken into small room along with another 4 inmates for a meeting with a Public Defender. As I felt sick, sort of claustrophobic, I was taken to the infirmary. After that I never heard from the lawyer again.

Days later I was visited by Ms. Morgan, a forensic social worker.

The TRIAL: Aug.17 early in the morning I was taken to what Elena now likes to call "the Injustice Bldg." At the courtroom Judge Leifman explained to me the 3 choices of: guilty, not guilty, and no contest. I chose the latter. Then the alleged victim, Mr. Escobar, an acquaintance of mine Mrs. Jacobson, and my friend Elena were called in.

SENTENCE:

*I was asked to apologize to Escobar.

*To pay $151.00 for attorney fees.. (A week later this was changed to 15 community hours, thanks to Elena's efforts).

*To attend to 8 classes of "anger control". (These classes had a cost of $100.00. Elena obtained a reduction of $50.00)

*And I was given a "Stay away order" of 200 feet from Escobar, anywhere in the USA and for the rest of my life, or risk being arrested again.

(Stay away from a man that I have only seen twice for a few minutes in my entire life? A man that means nothing to me. I don't understand.)

===

☐ IN THE CIRCUIT COURT OF THE ELEVENTH JUDICIAL CIRCUIT IN AND FOR DADE COUNTY, FLORIDA.
☒ IN THE COUNTY COURT IN AND FOR DADE COUNTY, FLORIDA

DIVISION		CASE NUMBER
☒ CRIMINAL	**STAY AWAY ORDER**	
☐ FAMILY	**NON-DOMESTIC VIOLENCE**	
☐ OTHER		*99. 4/10/9

STATE OF FLORIDA   VS.   CLOCK IN

Francis   *O Fao R*

PLAINTIFF(S)   DEFENDANT(S)

THIS CAUSE came before the Court to be heard, and the Court having been fully advised in the premises and having heard from the parties, it is hereby

ORDERED AND ADJUDGED that the above-named Defendant shall stay away from the victim(s) in this case, *Mr. Francis Escobar*, and shall have no contact with him/her in person, by telephone, and/or through any other individual. This shall include but is not limited to the victim's home and place of business.

DONE AND ORDERED in Dade County, Florida, this _____ day of ___8/7/99___, 19 _____

_____
Judge

Mi Casa - Tu Casa

We arrived at my house and I took Francis to the guest room, where the few things he owned were along with some new clothes I had bought for him. He took a shower and we went out for lunch. I showed him the neighborhood and the location of the South Dade Regional library, one he would visit for several years to come.

The next days we spent meeting the requirements imposed by the Court of 'In-Justice'. We visited the offices of the Advocate for anger management and a thrift shop for community service hours.

At the Advocate's he was interviewed by a Haitian sociologist who, after hearing the story of the incident, noticed the good manners and the academic level of Francis, shook his hand and told him to come to classes at least for...a few hours. In the meantime I was talking to another person in the office asking for a reduction of cost. At the thrift shop, they gave Francis his work schedule.

At home we had long talks and recorded songs and poems on cassettes. Also, he helped me with gardening and played a lot with Apolo and Allura.

Gardening   Mr. F. O'K.   Playing with Allura

In mid-October I accompanied Francis to the Social Security office, where he applied for disability benefits. To obtain this, he had to be seen by a psychiatrist, which was easier said than done. Francis went to Jackson Memorial Hospital and obtained a clinic card.
He made appointments with an ophthalmologist and a doctor of internal medicine. At the dentist's office they extracted two teeth.

Do not anyone believe that we were on a 'honeymoon.' Francis was angry with me as usual, though not as often. Sometimes he would sat at the dining table at night writing for hours and constantly smoking. I would come out of my room in the morning to find all the house lights on and the house filled with smoke like there was a fire. He didn't like that I wouldn't trust him to stay at home by himself, but I had already lived through one hurricane (Andrew, 1992) and I didn't need to relive that experience.

I continued working at West Dade Regional Library, and when I left for work Francis went on his bike around the neighborhood, visiting different shopping centers, the library, etc.

Francis - Allura - Apolo
Waiting for Elena to arrive from work.

Miami NewTimes - 1999

Published Incident of O'Keefe and Souto

On Thursday, Oct. 14, 1999 an article entitled "Book 'em Souto" written by Kathy Glasgow, was published by the Miami NewTimes. However, no copies of the newspaper were to be found in the vicinity around the West Dade Regional Library. Someone must have gotten up very early that morning to pick up all the copies, maybe someone who wanted to have photos of Francis...? Still, the paper got around.

Excerpts from the above mentioned article:

Francis O'Keefe is educated, erudite, and eloquent. He also has been homeless for the past twenty years. Recently the gray-haired man with questioning blue eyes has found refuge in a park that surrounds the West Miami-Dade Regional Library in Westchester. The library regulars seem to like O'Keefe, who is sober, well-mannered, and a whiz with the computer.

Souto has long been known for his outspoken antipathy toward loiterers and vagabonds. According to a 1994 El Nuevo Herald article, he once shocked county bureaucrats by declaring, "The more [homeless people] we have in jail the better."

"I was always impressed with his intelligence," adds Claire Jacobson, a woman who met O'Keefe at Matheson Hammock Park. She is one of the small but loyal collection of people who passionately believe O'Keefe is an innocent victim of a heartless politician.

One of the best responses we got came from one of Francis's acquaintances, Rita Mayer, who forwarded her email to me.

Subj: Your article on Francis O'Keefe
Date: 10/19/99 10:39:24 PM Eastern Daylight Time
From: AuroraLake
To: kathy_glasgow@miaminewtimes.com

Dear Ms. Glasgow:

Thank you for your insightful article on Francis O'Keefe's situation, and of Javier Souto's involvement. I am a special education teacher and an acquaintance of Mr. O'Keefe's and had been out of touch with him for several months. I met Elena about a week before your article came out, and through her accounts and your story, I was quite shocked to find out what had transpired. A year ago I had offered to help Mr. O'Keefe apply for disability, but he refused a psychiatric exam, which left my hands tied.

Up until my wedding last spring, I'd periodically visit him and provide him with food and toiletries, and a little bit of companionship, feeling this was all I could offer.

I've never met Mr. Souto and am outraged at his approach, but we both agree on one thing: We both want Mr. O'Keefe off the streets. The trouble is, Mr. Souto wants him in jail, and I want him in some kind of assisted living facility where he can get the personal and medical/psychiatric attention he needs.

Mr. O'Keefe is not a criminal; he is a victim of what anyone can clearly see is an irrationality which has robbed him of his ability to make reasonable life decisions, and which is henceforth keeping him on the streets in an ironic catch-22. Yes, Mr. O'Keefe is a charming, articulate, erudite gentleman, but his beliefs that "people are stealing from him psychically" and, as Elena reports, that he claims to be Great, are precisely what are keeping him on the streets and from getting the help he needs.

I am sure Mr. Souto does not care where Mr. O'Keefe goes, so long as it is not on the streets of his district. Sadly, he had the perfect opportunity permanently "rid" himself of Mr. O'Keefe the day of the alleged "assault and battery," but used a temporary, useless solution. Instead of having him arrested and sit in jail for almost a month, he or the photographer could have had him Baker Acted, which would have gotten the ball rolling for SSI and, eventually, a permanent home.

The fact that Mr. O'Keefe was assigned to" an anger management" class is absolutely ridiculous. I am disgusted with everyone from Mr. Souto to Mr. O'Keefe's court-appointed lawyer to the judge who handled this case, and everyone in between, and I am recommitting myself at this point, with the help of Elena, to hopefully finding a solution for Francis.

Thank you again for bringing this to the public's (and my) attention. If you can think of any way to facilitate Elena and my goal of helping Mr. O'Keefe, please contact me.

Incidentally, I find it interesting that the issue of last Thursday's Miami New Times, in which your article appeared, were curiously difficult to find in the Westchester area, which happens to be Mr. Souto's district.

Sincerely, Rita Mayer

Ironically, the same Thursday in October that the article was published coincided with the day Souto had his meeting with the residents of the 10th district in the WDR library. Carmen, another acquaintance of Francis, witnessed the meeting and then told me that almost all that the commissioner had spoken about was in reference to the issue of O'Keefe and, that he also hinted that I was the 'friend' of the indigent.

That day I was working at the desk right next to the main exit when Souto's meeting concluded. He came down from the second floor towards the exit. I followed him with my eyes and with a slight mocking smile. He walked straight without looking at me until he came right to the point where I was standing, and turned his head in my direction; in a second his rancorous gaze collided against my mocking expression. What a satisfaction!

The End of 1999

During the months Francis was living in my house there were ups and downs - there were days when he appreciated me more than anyone and other days when I was considered a pain. It got to the point that in a few occasions, either he chose to go back to the streets or I was forced to throw him out. Then the communication was by emails and we returned to make amends. This happened about three times.

Near my birthday, we were separated ... so I sent him an invitation:

Elena <epm15@yahoo.com> wrote: Happy Birthday to me !!! You are invited to my Party on: Sunday Nov.14,1999 From 3:30 pm to	Saturday, November 13, 1999 12:05 PM Elena, The most beautiful invitation card! I am so delighted! I will be the happiest to be there! love you. FRANCIS

Jose & Francis

1999 Nov.

Elena & Francis

Concentrating on the music that was playing on WTMI (classical radio station) and imagining conducting the orchestra. I do not know about musical conduction but as I watched him I thought he did really well. Another talent?

Francis – the Engineer

That's how I perceived him since he was very good at putting together things, "Do it Yourself" was invented for people like Francis. Definitely not for me. I can't stand instructions except number 1: Open the box.

While he was staying at my house he fixed a couple of things and showed me features that I didn't know my 3 years old lawn mower had.

For a while I had been looking for two nightstand tables for my bedroom. I wanted a simple table with no drawers and with certain measurements and, of course, I couldn't find them. I asked him if he thought we could build those tables and enthusiastically he said yes. First thing he did was to design it on paper according to my specifications, then Home Depot here we come. In a couple of days I had and still have my two tables.

Ask me if I would exchange them for two other made of the most precious wood with gold edges and I will just laugh and say: nope!

Throughout the years Francis, on his computer, designed several mechanisms to improve certain equipment, mainly bicycles. I have no idea if these inventions of his have a significant value or not but, we will never find out because although I have all those diagrams, I will never share them with anyone.

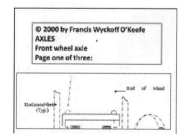

This is just a sample of his many papers. I am only showing half of the diagram.

On December 9, 1999 at WDR I was assigned to the Reference Desk from 6 to 7:30 pm. Suddenly before me, I saw Francis, who had come by bicycle from South Dade to visit, precisely the night that Souto had his "town meeting" in the library. I did not know whether to cry, scream, or laugh.

I gave him the keys to my car and $ 5. "Francis, Souto is about to get here, go and buy something to eat, and sit in my car until I leave at 9, please."

About 7 p.m. Souto and his entourage arrived. I guess he had seen Francis's bike (La Niña) parked in front. I heard him say he had a call to make and went to use the pay phone outside. A few minutes later, a policeman looking for O'Keefe showed up at my desk. I'll never forget that policeman ... he looked like a pig.

Police: O'Keefe is here?

I: Yes, somewhere around.

Police: He cannot be here when Escobar is here.

I: Oh, but I had understood it was only for 200 feet distance and this library has a lot more than that.

Police: I have orders to find him, where is he?

I: I do not know, so you go and find him.

He never found him.

A week later a position opened at South Dade Regional and I requested the transfer. WDR was about 15 miles and 30 minutes drive from my house and SDR was just two miles and seven minutes.

Conclusion:

After everything that happened, we forgot about Souto and Escobar.

As Francis said: "They are small people, without much significance. They are not 'true men.' True people live happy being him or her. Proud to be, not bitter for being. Does not victimized, but rather helps. He/she is intelligent, educated and a lover of truth." -*Francis O'Keefe, Jr.*

December 31, 1999

Happy New Century! I spent the 2000 New Year's Eve at home with Francis, Allura and Apollo.

The neighbors next door had a very Cuban fiesta - rice, black beans, yucca, pork roast, drinks and dancing music. We were invited. They thought of Francis as "American", but when the conga drums began and Francis asked me to dance, they all were surprised to see him move on the floor as a good salsa-man. We had a great time.

The 12 bells rang and a new century began. Francis and I hugged and went to greet Apolo and Allura that were watching us on the other side of the fence that separates my house from the neighbors.

Happy 2000!

New Century - New Life

The twentieth century didn't take with it neither Francis's craziness nor my patience. Therefore, we stayed the same - one day friends, and other days not so friendly. The year 2000 brought me a list of issues to be solved for Francis:
-Resolve the Social Security claim.
-Encourage him to be examined by doctors.
-Find him an apartment.
-Anything else that could come up.

Jan 8/2000 by Francis O'Keefe:

Sunday a doctor from the Social Security Administration came to examine me in regards to the claim of disability, or so it was said. This claim is on the base of what I experience that is not somatic, and which Elena has insisted it is neurological.
What I explained to him is that I hear voices, of people known and unknown, and that all are related to what I am and do and what happens around me, at times these right, at others wrong, and that there is one voice that takes hold of me and dominates, I then believing what it says; that I see also mentally; that I have a prodigious memory, talents, etc.
He pronounced me insane and left.

Once the medical certificate was obtained it should have been just a few days to get the request approved. The "bureau-crazy" did approve it, but didn't notify me. Three weeks went by without any notice.
I decided to go in person to the Social Security offices.
Many of the employees working in these offices have very arrogant attitudes. I do not know how they have come to believe that the funds they manage belong to them personally and that the applicants are simply beggars. At least that is the impression I got.

The woman who waited on me told me the case was approved but could not give Francis the check unless a psychiatrist would declare him able to manage his money. The other option: Someone to take responsibility, becoming the "payee."

"Ok, I'll take the responsibility," I said.

She looked at me as if I were a swindler and said: "The first check is a large sum."

"How much are we talking about?" I asked.

"$2,500 – two thousand five hundred," she answered.

"And that is what you call a large sum? Please!" I said sarcastically.

Again there were a series of forms to complete and return. Francis was not happy with the idea of having a payee, he did not want me to control him, but it was either I as a payee or him to a psychiatrist. And that's how I became a "payee."

Once one is approved for Social Security Supplement, one will also receive Medicaid health insurance and has the right to apply for food stamps, which until then was all that Francis had received.

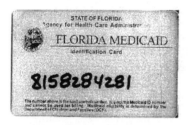 

On February 15, we received a check for $2,524. We opened a bank account: Elena Prieto for Francis W. O'Keefe, and I requested direct deposit. Beginning on April 1st the bank was to receive a monthly deposit of $512 - the amount allocated by Social Security. From that day on I had to keep Francis's financial records, for which I designed a control sheet.

We went shopping in order of importance: things for the bike, clothing and shoes for Francis and materials for drawing. He invited me to lunch at a Cuban restaurant.

Days later he got for me a pair of earrings, having taken into consideration my taste to combine gold and silver tones.

We went looking for an apartment. After several days, we found Cabana Club Apartments, a great location and just 1.5 miles from my house. Although far from being a luxurious building, it was well cared for, surrounded by a high fence with a security gate, parking for 300 cars, and an Olympic-size swimming pool. Only tenants 55 and over were admitted. The rent was reasonable. The apartment consisted of a living-dining room, kitchen with bar, bedroom, walk-in closet, bathroom with lights for heating, central air-conditioning and a terrace/balcony. It was perfect!

Cabanas had two apartments available, one on the 2nd floor and one on the 7th floor. Francis wanted the 7th but I insisted, for very good reasons, to take #201, which was in a corner right next to the fire escape, so he did not even need to take the elevator and, in case of fire, obviously from there to the street was nothing.

Francis wanted to live among the clouds.

Francis: "It is I who will live here. This one has a better view."

I: "Which view? All I see are the roofs of the whole neighborhood. Think of a fire or if the elevator breaks down."

Francis: "I prefer the 7th floor."

I: "Ok, Francis, but listen – do whatever pleases you, but if you go to the 7th floor I will never go visit you."

Francis: "Splendid!"

I said no more. We returned to the office. Francis returned the keys and very seriously told the office clerk: "I have decided to take #201."

Ahhhhhhhhh! Right there I gave him a hug. We did the paperwork.

On March 29 they gave us the keys and I placed the order for the installation of electricity and telephone services.

I helped him move and gave him all sorts of things I had at my house: bookcase, pillows, blankets, towels, kitchen utensils, two lawn chairs, a table, etc.

That was the last night Francis slept in my house.

Now he had his own address; his independence.

End of Homelessness. No more!

Francis W. O'Keefe - 19801 SW 110 Ct. Apt 201 – Miami, Fl. 33157

Francis was happy with his new life; but very annoyed because I was in control of his money. He called me the "administrator."

"No Francis, I'm more like your employee without pay." I responded.

Shortly after moving into the apartment, Francis began with complaints. They were unlikely things such as finding chewing gum on the carpet; he had left the window half opened and found it closed when he returned; a disk that he left on the table was gone, etc. Almost daily he had a claim. Someone was going into his apt. to do harm.

Luckily he did not accuse me although I had a key. He concluded by calling the police to file the complaints. After several calls, a sergeant (Frederick O. Poling, Jr.) took over the case "O'Keefe."

With Francis there was always something to be resolved. It was a never-ending story. Always something happened or there was something he needed. And to make matters worse, most of the time he would not tell me, because he was either angry at me or just would not tell me. The thing is that I was always solving or worrying.

At the end he showed up at the library. I don't remember where he said he had been.

In April, the Department of Children and Families wanted to reduce his food stamps benefits. I took care of it and it got resolved with an increase of $9 a month. Ay! If, I had been so efficient in solving the problems of vital importance that were to arise years later, perhaps this story would have had a different ending.

April 30, 2000

To Whom It May Concern:

I, Elena ████████ as a payee representative for Francis W.O'Keefe
with Soc. Sec. #265-███████, would like to provide you with
the following information:

After 20 years of being Homeless, Mr. O'keefe applied for SSI
and was approved to receive (due to his mental disability) the
amount of $512.00 a month and full Medicaid benefits.

In February 15, 2000 he received a check for $2524.00.
$1000.00 was deposited in a CD account with Nations Bank,
for future unforeseeable needs.
On April 1, 2000 he rented an unfurnished apartment at Cabana
Club, where a total of $900.00 was required to move in.
$125.00 was paid to FPL. and $47.00 to Bell South.
Any remaining of the money including a check for $512.00 that
he received in April 1, has been spent in clothing, bicycle
repairs, food, etc., for which I have all receipts.

In short, of the monthly................$512.00
apply for rent .... -435.00
estimated electricity .... - 35.00
    "   telephone .... - 15.00

He will have .... $ 27.00
to cover all his basic needs (toiletries, laundry, haircut,
bus fares, medical co-payments, etc.)

So, you go and figure it out!

I hope that his Food Stamps benefits not only remain the same,
but if possible be increased.

Sincerely,

Dear Francis,

You just turned one month as a resident of Cabana Club Apts. No more wandering and misery. Congratulations.

Love, Elena   5/2000

My dog, Apolo, was about 13 years old and was sick. One afternoon in the month of June I decided to end his misery by taking him to the vet to put him to sleep. I called Francis to help me carry him to my car and to accompany me.

Apolo was on the table, the doctor injected him as I was petting him. Within minutes the injection took effect. Francis was near me and for the second time I saw him with tears in his eyes. The first time I had seen him so emotional was when I gave him a picture of his father, which I had copied from one of Georgia's biographies. Upon seeing it, Francis' eyes filled with tears, had exclaimed, "Oh, it is my father."

Francis was a very noble man, a quality that I think the dogs detected. One of my neighbors had two German shepherds, who were trained to attack. On one occasion, Francis went out on my yard and they began barking in a scary way. Before I could yell to Francis, "Do not get close!" he had already leaned over the fence and was petting the dogs who were both standing on their two legs encouraging him to pet them, while Francis was saying to them, "What good dogs and how beautiful you are!"

But hey, was he Francis O'Keefe or Francis of Assisi?

15 Nov. 2000 Fiesta

Dear Francis.
Here is the
best looking
"Payee" and
your best friend.
Love,
SC.

Accidents and Incidents.

Little by little Francis filled his apartment with stuff he found here and there. He kept a steady diary of his comings and goings, which he wrote (sometimes in English, other times in Spanish) on his computer and saved on floppy disks. The details of these writings are over-whelming: One can say he wrote a detailed story of the simplest incident, thanks in part to his fantastic memory.

Here is a summary narrated by Francis:

ACCIDENT OF 21 MARCH 2002:
Florida Highway Patrol Case #02251542601

I reached the southwest corner of US1 and Marlin, travelling northward, and stopped and waited for the light to turn green to cross US1. I then began to cross Marlin on the crosswalk, and a small red car came over the crosswalk and hit me, I not having seen it. In the middle lane, next to the lane on which the red car travelled, was an automobile of a police aide, driven by a police woman. She said she did not see the accident, but she knew the light was red since she was stopped before the crosswalk and waiting for it.

A small report of the accident, giving only the names of those involved, and the insurance company of the driver of the automobile, and perhaps the license of the automobile, was given to me by the Miami-Dade police officer.

After being hit I felt dizzy when I got up. I asked to be taken by ambulance to Baptist Hospital; there I was examined and discharged.

I contacted the insurance company, State Farm, by which the driver is insured.

This accident happened in March. Francis was only slightly injured; the bike suffered more damage.

A case like this shouldn't take more than 45 days for a settlement between the insurance company and the injured party. Well, this case was closed in December, after my intervention in October, as Francis did not allow me to get involved earlier. I was the 'payee', the odious payee.

On December 6, Francis deposited in his own bank account a check for $2948.94. He quietly transferred $500 to my account, which I learned when I received my bank statement. That was my dear Francis, one day he would ignore me and on another day would give me a $500 gift.

Afluffy was a poodle I got from my sister back in 2000 when she and her family left for Europe on vacation. When they came back, they found Afluffy had gained weight and was a happy camper who now had a surrogate mother – Allura. So, Afluffy stayed with me.
As usual, both dogs loved Francis.

2003 - Vigilante

One Monday morning, Francis took a mini-bus that would take him to the library of Coral Reef. During the trip, the driver stopped and got out to buy a coffee. It was an opportunity to steal money from the ticket collection box that a young black guy took advantage of. When the driver returned, Francis informed him that he had been robbed, as he pointed to the offender. The driver looked seriously at Francis, said nothing, and continued driving.

The thief then went to Francis saying "that was none of your business" and began to beat Francis, who was sitting on one of the side benches, then Francis with a closed fist punched the guy on the testicles. The driver stopped the bus and opened the doors, allowing the offender to flee. The thief had also punched Francis on the face; for a few days he wore a hematoma on the upper left eye.

When Francis arrived at his stop found that there had been an accident and the police were there. He addressed them and told them about the incident. The officers took note and later the guy was caught.

I'm sure that with Francis's eidetic memory he was able to give the policemen a very accurate description of the delinquent.

Days later Francis received a notice from the State Attorney:

He forgot about the incident and kept going with his life.

Where is O'Keefe?
FROM:Elena PM
TO:Poling Jr. Frederick O. (MDPD)
Friday, February 11, 2005 10:19 AM
Hello Sargent,
I went by Cabana apts this morning and nobody has seen Francis in the last 3 days. We went inside his apt and lights and heater were on, and his 2 bicycles were there.I called Baptist and Deering Hospitals and Nada. Could he be in jail? I just hope he is Ok, wherever he is. Tomorrow is his Birthday. Thanks

---

From: Elena PM
Sent: Friday, February 11, 2005 8:54 PM
To: Poling Jr. Frederick O. (MDPD)

Subject: case closed

Sgt.,The police were at my house when Francis called from South Miami Hospital. Some kidney infection and said he's been sleeping for the last 3 days.

I was so happy to hear from him and to learn he was fine that I couldn't show any anger for not getting in touch with me earlier.

But soon as the smile fades away from my face, I'm going to kill him before he gives me a heart-attack, so it will be like a self-defense, right? Anyways I have been in touch with the Police so many times because of O'Keefe, that by now I probably have a Criminal Record. Now I understand why you transfer to the Airport.Well, one more time THANKS ! Have a great day, Elena

---

FROM: Poling Jr., Frederick O. (MDPD)
TO:Elena PM'
Sunday, February 13, 2005 6:35 AM
 Elena:
 I am so glad you were able to find Francis. Tell him I said hello. No I didn't transfer to the Airport to get away from Francis. LOL. It is a pleasure to assist you, CALL ME anytime, I am always here to help. Rick   Miami-Dade Police Department

Written by Francis – minor editing by Elena

==

Unjust and Offensive Arrest in Delray Beach. – Baker Act.

On Sunday, May 15, 2005, I went to West Palm Beach by Tri-Rail. I disembarked; thought of not continuing, feeling too tired. I took bus No. 1 of Palm Beach County Transit going South. On Sundays bus No 1 only travels to Del Ray Beach, the last stop just past Atlantic Avenue, on US1 southbound.

On US1 I sought to catch another bus, still not knowing that none went by on Sunday going further south, then I realized what the bus driver had meant, and that I had to walk to Miami-Dade.

I began to walk towards the South; a long distance awaited me.

As I walked I was feeling physically ill. My stomach felt upset, I was limping, limping because of my right foot injured, it slightly twisted by the car accident, and pains in my legs. I hoped I could ask a policeman or woman for help, to take me to a hospital.

After a few blocks, a police car drove slowly past me, and turned at the corner, ominous. In a short moment the same or another came and stopped slightly ahead of me. I said to the driver I was glad he had come for I needed help, thinking of being taken to a hospital because of my physical problems. (I have gone to the ER of three in the last six months, spending five days in one.)

But it turned out that he began to ask me the questions asked of someone suspected of committing a crime, which many of the police ask because they want to, without any explanation.

A second policeman arrived. His surname is Dennis. Dennis said he believed me when I said I had gone to West Palm Beach by Tri-Rail. I nevertheless showed to him the ticket. The police report states the name of the first policeman is D. Rotondi.

My backpack was searched. Floppy disks in it were opened, after asking for my permission, which I may have not given and may not have been respected, futile probably to have refused. Policeman Dennis was the one who took the floppy disks to the police car he drove, and he asked me, insinuatingly, if there was anything pornographic in them, or so I understood by the way he asked, not finishing the sentence: "There is nothing in them...?" He made a copy of one writing, saying it was confusing.

The other policeman, Rotondi asked me "Where is your computer?" I answered "At home." My clothes and body were not searched. I was asked by Dennis if I heard voices! Why?

Arrest was made, several times said it was not an arrest, but in public view, I handcuffed regardless of it said several times I was not arrested, as reason for the handcuffing that it is departmental policy to handcuff whomsoever is placed inside a police car!

I refused to go, but both grabbed me by the arms. I was handcuffed, handcuffed by the use of force as I said, placed inside the police car, driven to, South County Mental Health, where I had to stay for most of the night until transported to another, the latter Oakwood, in Mangonia.

The policeman, Rotondi, drove to South County Mental Health behind a series of buildings about one block from said hospital.

The policeman, Dennis, said it is suspicious to carry a backpack. Suspicious of what? Several times, Rotondi, insisted on asking if I was homeless, and several times he spoke to me as if I were.

It was about 7:00 p.m. Upon reaching the first hospital, South County Mental Health, I suffered from the handcuffs too tight and the lack of air, and told the policeman, Rotundi. He said it would only be a moment, a moment that extended and extended, I telling him my suffering, receiving the same answer, and the same long wait, three times.

This policeman in front of the hospital and both of us out of the car addressed me by Francis several times. I said several times my name is O'Keefe. He looked at the paper on which my name was written and said "It is not Francis?", as if he had made a mistake. I said he had to address me by O'Keefe, that we were not friends. He continued calling me Francis.

The treatment of me at the first hospital was good, pleasant, and amicable, with estimation even. There something funny happened. I asked for a pencil or pen to write the phone number of the cellular telephone of Elena as she spoke to me over the telephone, and it was said no one, i.e., inmate, could have a pencil or a pen, obviously for protection. (1)

Time later the nurse came to ask me to sign a paper, and I said I could not use a pen or pencil. And she asked, seriously, "How come someone with a Master of Arts diploma cannot use a pen or a pencil?" The woman who had said that to me smiled at the comical of the situation.

A few hours afterwards I was transferred to a hospital in Mangonia, Oakwood. Here the treatment was also good, except at the beginning. At the lobby I was feeling very cold because of the air conditioner, I always suffering much from the cold weather, and the black female nurse did not let me obtain a jacket from my backpack, saying she had to search it first and never did, and as with the policeman Rotondi I had to wait and wait and wait, this time not suffocating but cold.

She asked me what my sexual orientation was. I answered heterosexual that I am a true man, and she gave me a disdainful, unbelieving look as if it could not be true. (2)

At Oakwood, they gave me a little, white pill "for high blood pressure". Dr Terralonge in Miami, of JMH, had said a short time before that I had high blood pressure, first time this was said to me.

The doctor at Oakwood, Dr. Kim, asked me a few questions, the date, I off by one day, which he dismissed as normal, who was president of the United States, the one before (which I should have answered "Bush." again) His intention, a good joke by which he offered me the opportunity to prove I am sane.) He asked me if I had desired to kill myself, to kill someone (which I answered by saying I had gone to war). If I heard voices,(to which I answered that I think with words too), and he stopped me and proceeded. At the end he asked, rapidly, series of arithmetic problems, which I also answered rapidly.

Dismissing the report by the police of I insane after testing me, Dr. Kim, advised me to not go about walking, thus a reference to the abuse by the police towards the ones in poverty.

I was given a courtesy ticket for the Tri-Rail to return to Miami.
-Francis Wyckoff O'Keefe, M.A.

==

1- I did not know where Francis had gone on Sunday, but as always, when Monday came without knowledge about him I began to make inquiries over the phone. By then I was an expert in seeking and finding Francis.

Once I found him in Delray Beach hospital and heard his story, I got furious. I remember telling the nurse that they could not have him there against his will since he had committed no act of violence; therefore it was illegal. I demanded he be discharged immediately.

2- When Francis told the nurse "he was a true man" he was not being "macho." Francis called a true man, one with integrity and one who is just.

DELRAY BEACH POLICE DEPARTMENT

STATUS REPORT

☐ Status Form
☒ Continuation Form

☐ 1 Number of Suspects, Victims, & Witnesses

Page 3 of 3

Incident Number	DATE	OFFICER ID NUMBER	BACK UP NUMBER	Other Annotations
05-12954	5/15/05	893	C121	SUBJECT BAKER ACTED

STATUS INFO

Sex Male	Person Type: Baker Act	Last / First / M.I	DOB 02/ 12 /39	Age 66
Race White	O'Keefe / Francis / W		
Height 5-8 1/2"	Occupation Retired	☐ Employer ☐ School ☐ Drug Rehab	Social Security Number
Weight 180			
Build Thin			
Eyes Blue	Residence Address 19801 SW 110 Ct. #201, Miami	STATE FL ZIP 33157 PHONE (305) 969-3766
Hair White	Business Address N/A	STATE ZIP PHONE ( )
Complex Light		

STATUS INFO

☐ Owner has all Keys ☐ Released
LOCATION WHERE: ☐ Recovered ☐ Stored

TOWED BY: ___ AUTHORIZED BY: ___

While I was patrolling around the 200 block of SE 5th Ave, I noticed a man on the sidewalk having difficulties walking. I pulled my patrol car up to him and asked if he was all right. The subject, later identified as Francis O'Keefe, told me he was not doing too well. The subject stated he had several medical conditions, including sore legs, gingivitis, a fungus infection and other ailments. Francis stated that he took a train from Miami to West Palm Beach but had no way of getting back home to Miami. Francis said that he was going to walk home. He also said that he hears voices in his head regularly on a daily basis. A consented search of the subject's backpack turned up several floppy discs with unusual letters about the voices Francis was hearing.

Francis was Baker Acted and transported to South County Mental Health for further evaluation.

☐ Check here if it appears that the person has drug or alcohol involvement in addition to mental illness (does not disqualify for Baker Act admission)

_____
Signature of Law Enforcement Officer

5/15/05	7:49 PM	am (pm)
Date (mm/dd/yyyy)	Time	

Ofc. D.Rotondi
_____
Printed Name of Law Enforcement Officer

Delray Beach Police Department
Full Name of Law Enforcement Agency

893
_____
Badge or ID Number

05-12954
_____
Law Enforcement Case Number

By Authority of s. 394.463(2)(a) 2, Florida Statutes
CF-MH 3052a. Jan 98 (obsoletes previous editions)

(Mandatory Form)

BAKER ACT CONFIDENTIAL

MAY 17 2005

Many difficult situations have been resolved thanks to this law. Also, because of this law many abuses have been committed.

O'Keefe & Healthcare.

At age 65, in 2004, Francis began to receive Medicare benefits. From day one I asked him not to join an HMO. That way he could go to any doctor and hospital he wanted, since he also had Medicaid insurance. So, it could be said that he had complete coverage.

The point is that there are plenty of misleading medical centers and HMOs who like to meet in communities where retired people reside and who are not very enlightened in the Business of Health. During these meetings small meals and cheap gifts (key rings, sunglasses, hats, etc. "Made in China") are given to the audience. Then they try to sell them the membership to the HMO offering "free" services such as transportation, eyeglasses, dental care, and even free breakfasts at some of their medical centers.

One day Francis signed up with one of those HMO's and then they covered almost *nada*! I called the Medicare office and they were able to reinstate Francis to his free Medicare.

Francis lived in total ambivalence in regard to doctors and hospitals. During the years 2000-2005 he was admitted several times. He had double hernia surgery and surgery of the carotid arteries. He wouldn't tell me before each hospitalization and each surgery, but did call me later. Then I had to go to discuss the matter with the doctors, who did not always detect Francis's schizophrenia.

It was a constant struggle. When a doctor told him what he wanted to hear ... it was a good doctor, and when a doctor did not pay much attention to many of his 'sufferings', sometimes normal things like sweating even when it was cold, then it was a bad doctor who might want to hurt him further. I was in the middle of all this, able sometimes to help and other times not.

Francis had his neurological or psychiatric problem; that has been established. However, some doctors and nurses lacked the basic knowledge of psychology to understand a patient with delusions; and also lacked the neurons, or hormones or whatever it is that manages the feelings of compassion. So, there we were.

2005 South Beach

October 2005 - Francis was notified by the Miami Beach Housing Authority that his request for affordable housing had been approved. The building was called Rebecca Towers and was located next to the marina of South Beach. This time Francis went to reside in a studio on the 13th floor. Rent: $135 monthly.

I was the one who had to deal with the moving. I hired the man that mowed my yard and had a pick-up truck. After four trips from Cabana to Rebecca we were done near midnight. The next day I called the electricity, telephone, and internet companies to make the transfers.

This change of domicile was a disaster; it hurts us tremendously, especially Francis. Yes, now he had more money to spend and did spend it, but a storm was approaching us.

When Francis lived five minutes from my house, I could easily assist him with all his affairs. Also, we could visit each other and have coffee either at my home or at his apartment. South Miami Heights, where both of us resided and where I still reside, is a middle class neighborhood with all public and commercial services and access to the expressway and the U.S. 1 highway. South Beach, on the other hand is mainly a tourist area; everything costs more and finding parking is a drama. And now we resided 20 miles away from each other.

As Francis was saving money on rent I was spending more on gas and tolls to visit him. And what about the 30 to 45 minutes it took me to get to South Beach? What a deal!

We started the year 2006 well.

Francis was very skilled at assembling and disassembling gadgets. He was fascinated by bicycle tools, digital devices and flashlights!

One day he picked up a Fax – Scanner - Copier from the trash in his building. Then, he contacted the manufacturer by email requesting the operating instructions.

Within a few days the equipment was already connected to his computer and Francis was sending faxes.

The studio in which he lived was large but not enough to have three phones; however, he had one on his desk, another near the bed, another in the kitchen. All connections were made by him.

Every time I went to visit, he would show me one of his inventions. Jokingly I told him that one day we were going to get electrocuted. But everything worked and he enjoyed all that entanglement of cables.

The Storm Hit

FROM: francisokeefe@bellsouth.net

TO: epm15@yahoo.com

Thursday, September 28, 2006 5:18 PM

I have cancer.

I am in pain. I must go to Md. on the 1st of October to begin treatment, but I am in pain, and the insurance company, WellCare, contrary to what the agent said I was to receive, will not provide transportation to the offices of doctors. I am hardly able to move. My apartment is dirty. I need a small seat to place on the bathtub to bathe; I have the money to buy it but cannot go anywhere. The same with other things. I twice went by bus to places but the trips left me in worse state.

From that day on things started to become really difficult. Francis's schizophrenia did not help at all with cancer. Wellcare HMO was good for nothing. And, I had less time off to attend to Francis. I had my own personal problems and my job with the public library, and Francis was no longer five minutes from my house but a good one-hour's drive away. And on top of that was Francis's habit of getting mad at me now often than usual – not taking my calls, no replying to my emails.

I got in contact with Magnolia, the social worker of the building, to keep me informed of any emergency during her working hours:

9 a.m. to 5 p.m. After those hours…

Oncologo
FROM: francisokeefe@bellsouth.net
TO:epm15@yahoo.com
Thursday, October 19, 2006 2:01 AM

Well, I went to the oncologist. Made appointments with other special-ists to do certain things to me and start treatment. They're going to put something in me semi-permanent through which the drugs will be administered like an IV, rather than injected into the veins. Will be made through an operation under local anesthesia. I think they also will do another biopsy. He said that the growth arose where there was a double hernia, which caused confusion among some seven doctors, it is also lymphoma.

Oxycodone was prescribed, I take this as if it was water I said, he understanding that it is necessary to take.

FROM:Elena PM
TO:Francis O'Keefe
Thursday, October 26, 2006 1:57 AM

I want to spend this Sunday with you.

Help you with the apartment; cook for you; and for you to tell me everything related to your health and what is being done or what can we do to overcome this evil.

Nobody gives me information because you have not given permission.
I'm tired of calling doctors, Social Workers, etc.
I am the only person who believes in you and who really cares for you.
I do not want you to feel alone in this situation.

I have always been with you, even if we were fighting.

And I'll always be, like it or not. Elena

Francis was being treated at Mount Sinai Hospital by an excellent oncologist, Dr. Mike Cusnir, since he had been diagnosed with lymphoma cancer.

The problem was that Francis had not undergone treatment. Although suffering intense pains, which were only relieved by taking dozens of pills, he had wasted time continually postponing treatment, simply because he was alone and terrified of the therapies. I contacted the doctor to explain the peculiar situation of Francis and promised to convince him and accompany him when the time for chemotherapy came.

On Wednesday, November 15th (my birthday) I celebrated aboard a cruise ship that took me to the Western Caribbean. I had previously reserved and paid for the trip.

A week later, back in Miami, I drove at noon to South Beach to attend with Francis an appointment with Dr. Cusnir.

From: Elena PM
Sent: Friday, December 01, 2006 1:55 PM
To: Mike Cusnir, MD
Subject: O'Keefe Case
Dr. Cusnir,
It was a pleasure to meet you personally. Hopefully you'll never lose the human quality that you seem to have and that is not abundant among most professionals.
O'Keefe has overwhelmed me with the issue of the "bone marrow" test. He says you said it was "very painful."
If we can do it with general anesthesia, he is going to undergo without resistance. About 18 months ago, he was operated on a carotid at Baptist. They started with local anesthesia and had to end with general because he was very upset.
Remember there is a mental disability that prevents him to react and understand the way you or I would do it.
Always grateful for your attention. Elena

FROM:Mike Cusnir, MD

TO:Elena PM
Friday, December 1, 2006 2:26 PM

It is a pleasure for me. If he does not want to have a biopsy of medulla is ok, we still could start treatment. But more important is the PET scan that he also canceled.Try to convince him and I will see him as soon as possible.

Dr. Cusnir gave us the referral for primary care physician Dr. Cohn, who needed to send it to Wellcare HMO for approval. Francis was associated with this inefficient HMO. Then began the drawbacks with the 'bureaucratic' health system so I sent the following fax to all the doctors and assistants that appear here. I felt totally frustrated.

Att. Dr. Cusnir & Elizabeth –Nurse	Att. Dr. Cohn & Madeline –Secretary	Att. Dr. Paramo & Ada - Secretary

Ref. Francis W. O'Keefe SS – 265- XX- XXXX

11/22/06- Dr. Mike Cusnir gave Prescription for Port Placement by Dr. Juan Paramo.

Prescription had to go first through Dr. David Cohn –Primary.

Dr. Cohn has to contact Wellcare 888-888-9355 for approval.
However, Dr. Paramo is not affiliated with Wellcare

Therefore, Dr. Cohn needs to contact Wellcare at 866-389-9669 or Outpatient Authorization.

Or, Dr. Paramo should ask Wellcare to contact Linda at Mount Sinai 305-674-3977 to work on a "Letter of Agreement"

As of Friday, December 08, 2006 nothing has really been resolved. Francis is getting sicker as time goes by.

Finally, we started with the therapies. I went with Francis to most of the treatments. They had placed a port near his collarbone through which the medication was introduced.

==

"It is pain what worried me. As I told the oncologist, I am tired of having pains. If I die I will cease to experience pain.
But I think there is a chance of being cured." - *Francis*

From: Elena PM
 Date: 2006/12/19 Tue PM 11:18:55 EST
To: Francis O'Keefe
Subject: Importante

Dear Francis,

As your Assistant/Secretary it is my job to remind you the following:

1- Please READ the folder you were giving tonight by the ChemoTechnician

2- The medication you took at 9PM should have been taken with Milk, not on an empty stomach. This is not a pain killer but, a Hormone to balance the White Blood Cells. Only 2 pills every 24 hours.

3- Get Cash to finish the Drying Laundry and $25.00 for Ana (maid) who is going to go by on Wednesday 12/20/06 around 3pm

4- Also on 12/20/06 you have an appt. with Cusnir for another medication.Ask him for a meeting with the Nutritionist.

And for their Social Worker (Irene) to get you some Home Assistant.

Also, about Transportation (back and forth) for the next Chemotherapy.

Well, I hope that you liked the "re-organization" I did in the apt and all the other services rendered.

I hope you are not firing me. I need this job - just like I need a hole in the head.

That's it for today - a very long day! Un abrazo, Elenita

December 21, 2006
Elena,
I just wanted to write you a handwritten letter.
I love you much.
I think you're the only person that has helped me.
Francis

FROM: FRANCIS O'KEEFE

TO: epm15@yahoo.com

Monday, December 25, 2006 7:48 AM

Now it is 6:10 a.m., of Christmas Day. I need your physical presence, as silly as it may sound it is like a metaphysical cure, if it is not. Pains continue in my face, right side. Physical presence of someone good, who loves us and whom we love, aids enormously in all, for we aid one another. It is a metaphysical or religious occurrence, by which we are enormously aided and cured. We need one another. Bad company destroys, it steals, it murders, good company builds, protects and provides.

Today is Christmas. Merry Christmas I wish to you, although I do not know how I so ill. I wish you would come here again today, to help me feel better: you cure me, even physically by going to get medicines. I know this is to impose on someone overburdened, but I am not being an ill behaved child, as you know, and while it is not just your presence, your presence helps me enormously. I then also have someone to speak with about things that interest both. Thank you for rushing to buy Maalox. It was great. I thank you very much for watching over me. It made me feel protected, as it in reality was. You were much concerned.

Thank you too for the things you bought for me.

2007 – Cancer Cured

From: Elena PM
Sent: Monday, January 01, 2007 11:41 PM
To: Mike Cusnir, MD
Subject: O'keefe esta muy mal

Dear Doctor,

I'll be as brief as possible.
Today 1st. of January I visited Francis and I found him extremely
weak. He has lost almost 50 pounds in 3 months.
We went to a Burger King (he who always had a very good appetite)
only ordered a chocolate milkshake, after much insistence of mine.
He says he's disgusted with food, everything tastes bad. He eats
almost nothing, and always feels very cold.
Lately gets confused and forgets things. This never happened before;
though a bit crazy, he always had a very good memory.
What is going on with him?
Is his cancer really curable?
I am very concerned and very sad. I want to help as much as possi-
ble. I await your reply.
Thank you for your attention and for your help.
Elena

RE: O'keefe esta muy mal
FROM:Mike Cusnir, MD
TO:Elena PM
Tuesday, January 2, 2007 8:43 AM
Hello Dona Elena
These are side effects of chemotherapy and will gradually disappear.
The idea is to cure Don Francis.
I see him today anyway and I'll have the nutritionist see him.
We'll talk.
Mike

FROM:Elena PM
TO:Mike Cusnir MD
Sunday, January 7, 2007 10:58 PM
Report O'Keefe
Hello Doctor, Today Sunday I spent all morning with Francis.
I found him much better. He's weighing 140 lbs.
I cleaned his apt. a little, washed his clothes, and we went to
Publix and made a healthy purchase
I left him happy.
He is eating a little more, taking Ensure daily and sleeps a lot,
which I think is good.
As of Feb. 1st he'll be on Free Medicare. No more Wellcare.
I am aware that you must have a lot of patients, especially less
problematic than Francis, but, I wanted to give you this report as
an "update".
I will not take more of your valuable time. Always very grateful,
Elena

FROM: francisokeefe@bellsouth.net
TO: epm15@yahoo.com
Monday, January 8, 2007 11:43 PM

I had a very nice thought about you dear Elenita, but I could not
retain it in my memory. You really have helped me in every way.
How I wish you were with me now. You should be here not only
to clean the house, dishes, cooking. (ha,ha,ha.)
I would like that our phone conversations were also in person.
Your thoughts about me are beautiful. I read the e-mail.
Thanks a lot for the photos. I am delighted to have them.
Until tomorrow at 10:00 a.m.
A kiss, Francis

Toward the end of March the cancer had subsided and almost disappeared. Francis continued his routine of purchasing gadgets and now he had another two bicycles for which to buy lights, mirrors, etc. By this time he had lost "La Niña" which he left forgotten on a bus.

He was also angry with me; this time for several months, and the reason was basically because I was the 'payee.' He got in touch with me only through emails and only to ask me briefly to make a money transfer. I called him almost every night, and as soon as he heard my voice he said, "No!" and hung up.

I kept calling him every other day. For me it was enough to hear his "No!" to know he was all right.

Francis's Accusations & the New Year

In the month of June, Francis wrote to the Florida Department of the Elderly, complaining that I was not giving him the much-needed money to cover his expenses. This resulted in an investigation that caused me to lose working hours to attend an interview with the Social Security office.

FROM:Elena PM
TO:Francis O'Keefe
Wednesday, June 6, 2007 4:34 PM
Francis,
I just received a call from the Elderly Affairs in reference to a letter you sent to them. Would you send me a copy of that letter, so I could have a better idea of what the hell they are talking about?
Thanks, Elena

Francis never replied, nor did I see the letter. However, what bothered me the most was not Francis's complaint, but the way in which the officer (Elderly Affairs) who called me spoke and threatened me. I e-mailed my complaint to the director of the department. I received an automatic reply saying that within five working days I was going to get an answer. They never attended to my complaint. Bureaucrats!

FROM:Elena PM
TO:information@elderaffairs.org
Thursday, June 7, 2007 3:46 PM
E. Douglas Beach, Secretary Florida Department of Elder Affairs

Sir, I am addressing you in regards to a complaint I have toward an employee of your department. Unfortunately, I was unable to get her full name but it was something that started with "White......". She called me yesterday, June 6, 2007 at 3:53 pm from telephone # 850-922-8305. Her call was pertaining to a Letter of Complaint against my persona. This letter was sent by Mr. Francis O'Keefe and had something to do with his moneys from Social Security of which I am the "payee".This Ms. White.....began by asking me question after question in a very aggressive manner. Also, she wouldn't allow me to reply properly.

At one point I said "You know ma'am, I don't want to have this conversation over the phone..." - meaning that I preferred to discuss this matter on a personal interview. However, she did not let me finish my sentence and interrupted me, with an almost neurotic attitude, saying something like: "Well, I'm going to report you to the General Inspector in Washington, blah, blah, blah..." and Sir, I just hanged up on her.

I have tried to contact Mr. O'Keefe by email and by phone asking him about his letter to the Elder Affairs Dept., but he is avoiding me as usual.Therefore, I am not exactly sure what his complaint is about this time.Whatever the complaint was, it seems that this Ms. White.... believed every word of his letter and instantly became Mr. O'Keefe's advocate. Her position with the department is not of my concern; nevertheless, she needs to be taught that there is something called: Good manners. Also that: There are two sides to a coin. & Things are not always what they seem.

Allow me to add that at the time of this call I was on my lunch break. I suffer from high blood pressure and this woman's impertinent call upset me to the point that I ended up not eating and drinking a Linden tea instead.

I'll be happy to cooperate with any investigation conducted by any USA Government Dept. as long as I am treated with respect and be considered "Innocent, until proven guilty beyond any reasonable doubt." Thank you for your attention. Sincerely, Elena PM

"COMMITTED TO EXCELLENCE"

7/09/07

Received
7/12/07

Elena Prieto
19902 SW 121ª Ave
Miami, Fl 33177

Dear Mrs. Prieto:

Please be advised that the Department of Children and
Families received a report about suspected Abuse, Neglect,
Exploitation or Special Conditions.

It is imperative that you contact our office as soon as
possible to discuss the allegations that have been raised.

In order to complete our investigation, I need all the
documentation/information you have related to
this matter.

Thank you for your prompt attention.

Sincerely,

Rosalyn Wooten, Protective Investigator
(305) 377- 5637

Case #2007- 403001

Cell 305-319·1902

Florida Department of
Children and Families

Rosalyn Wooten
Adult Protective Investigator

Adult Protective Services
401 NW 2nd Avenue, Suite S-417, Miami, Florida 33128
Tel. (305) 377-5599c (305) 808-6253

*The Department of Children and Families is committed to working in partnership with local
communities to ensure safety, well-being and self-sufficiency for the people we serve.*

The only reason for which they show interest in the case was because
there was money involved. Otherwise, where were they when Francis
was living on the streets?

The appointment at the Social Security office took place with Mr. Rivas, who rudely greeted me, his attitude based on what Francis might have written and what Ms. White… (Elderly Affairs) reported.

As Mr. Rivas asked me for documentation, I quietly began to show him bank records, expense receipts, photos, emails, the NewTimes article, etc.

And finally, I asked if he wanted proof of all working hours I had lost, in order to accompany Francis to doctors, as well as gasoline expenses, tolls, parking, etc. If we were to add all I had spent since I met him back in 1998, it would have amounted to approximately $1500 of my own money.

Although what I said was very true, I knew that it did not count, but I couldn't help being sarcastic.

 When People Need Help Managing Their Money

Social Security's Representative Payment Program provides financial management for the Social Security and SSI payments of our beneficiaries who are incapable of managing their Social Security or SSI payments.
Generally, we look for family or friends to serve in this capacity.
When friends and family are not able to serve as payee, Social Security looks for qualified organizations to be a representative payee.

During my interview with Mr. Rivas, I told him about my possible resignation as a payee for Mr. O'Keefe and asked him how soon S.S.A. could find an agency that will take care of Francis. The answer was that there was not such a thing. If I gave up, the SSA would immediately stop the monthly payments. Which meant homelessness. Therefore, the poster on the wall saying otherwise was simple bullshit.
If I'd had Francis's "Expeditionary Medal" with me, I would have thrown it at Mr. Rivas.

FROM:Elena PM

TO:Francis O'Keefe

Tuesday, July 24, 2007 7:56 PM

Francis, As your payee I have been informed that you have to keep in touch with me regularly, and as I told you a while ago, I need to document how you spent your moneys.

Also, I keep receiving AARP & Medicare Summary Notices. There is nothing I can do with any of this information since you will not inform me anymore about your well-being I have no idea what medications or doctors you use.

It's been more than 3 months that you have refused to answer my calls and you only email me when is "pay day". And on top of that you reported me to the Elder Affairs dept. and caused an unnecessary and unfair investigation.

You think I'm kidding when I said that THEY don't care and will easily put you back on the streets, unless you comply with their demands - like - a doctor's note: *that you are capable of managing your own money.*

I am absolutely sick - tired - fed up with this PAYEE business.

Do something! or I'm quitting you my friend.

Of course I did not keep my threat. And of course I was exonerated of all charges.

November 2007 - We smoked the peace pipe.

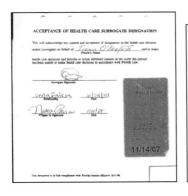

Francis was admitted to Cedars Hospital. As always I had to mediate between the doctors and him. Somehow, he agreed to sign a document providing me with the authority to decide for him in case he could not do it.

31 December 2007

Francis came to my house on the 31st. About 9 p.m. we went in my car to a Checker's on US1, which has outdoor seating. We ate burgers, fries, and soda. From there we went to Dadeland, where we parked the car and took the Metro-Rail to Bayfront Park to welcome the New Year.

I would have never dared, to do that traveling alone at that hour of the night, but accompanied by Francis I felt completely calm. It was not as if he was a Bruce Lee, but I was sure that, in case we were attacked by ruffians, Francis would have either confronted them or decided that we should flee. In any case, he would not have abandoned me.

It was the first and last time for both of us, coming to this site for this celebration. I had a bottle of cider and two plastic cups. Sitting on a seawall facing the bay, we saw the fireworks, the rise of the "Big Orange" and participated in the traditional countdown: 10-9-8-7-6-5-4-3-2-1 - Happy New Year!!!

Of the many past New Year's Eve celebrations, there are few that I remember fondly. This 2007 with Francis is definitely one of them.

Beginning of the End

We started the year well. On February 9, we went on a half-day cruise. On the return trip we were seating in the pool area by the bar when some Latin music began and we went dancing. Other passengers photographed us and applauded.

On his 69th Birthday (Feb. 12) I invited Francis for lunch to an Outback restaurant in Miami Beach. Francis enjoyed a good meal, mainly because he didn't know how to prepare even a canned soup. That day we shared a dessert. Then we strolled through the marina.

Our last photo together.

Before continuing with the story of Francis I have to talk a bit about my personal life, especially about those first 7 months of 2008. My mother was diagnosed with Alzheimer's in 1999 and in 2002 came to live at my house. My siblings helped me with a monthly allowance to cover expenses, including the employment of assistants to care for her. However, Alzheimer's is not a joke; it is a progressive disease that begins with memory loss and escalates to confusion, aggression, depression and loss of skills. Well, apart from my domestic responsibilities, my dogs and my job I had the great responsibility of ensuring the health care and comfort of my mother. And, last but not least, Francis and his problems, some imaginary and others really serious. Until 2008 I was able to balance the situation with the help of Xanax, by the way. But that 2008 ...

I was temporarily transferred to work at West Kendall Regional Library, which was quite far from my home as well as from Francis. Whenever an emergency arose with my mother or Francis, it was an ordeal driving to get home or to a hospital.

In that library one worked in an environment charged with negative energy, in the words of many. The 'manager', whose professional knowledge could be questioned and even the English she spoke was very poor, was accustomed to being flattered by her staff, and that is something I never learned to do.

She, like the rest of the staff with whom I worked, were all very religious but, more than once I was asked: "Why you care so much for this man's troubles when he is not your father or your brother or your husband?" Amen.

Therefore, I was reprimanded several times because of "my personal problems." I did put an end to this, though too late, in July when I took a leave of absence for 30 days.

This is all I wanted to say about myself, to tell the difficulties I had to deal with and the vicissitudes I endured in those first seven months.

From here on ...

In March, Francis began to feel ill. As usual, he made wrong decisions about his health. He was highly intelligent and an intellectual but in physiology he was lost. If we add to that the schizophrenia, which in this particular case did not allow him to discern among his different ailments, the result was tragic.

At Cedars Hospital, he was hospitalized on April 17, 2008 because of pains in his lower back, abdomen, and left thigh. There he stayed for four days and was discharged without a real diagnosis.

===

"At Cedars, now purchased by UMHC, I went last Thursday, April 17, 2008, because of pains in my lower back and abdomen and left thigh. Today is Monday, April 21, 2008. In those four days twice I was given X-Rays, but the results were not told to me. Blood samples were taken for analysis, and the results not told to me." - Francis

===

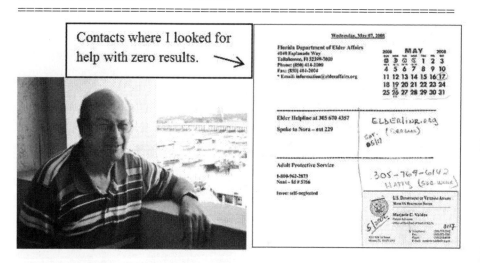

Contacts where I looked for help with zero results.

FROM: francisokeefe@bellsouth.net
TO: epm15@yahoo.com
Saturday, May 3, 2008 11:46 AM

Today I was discharged from Mount Sinai in pain.

Terminal Cancer

Dr. Cusnir informed us that there was no cure for Francis; his life estimate was 6 months, during which he would prescribe medication to relieve the pains. I do not know what Francis felt, because I do not know what I felt after that final diagnosis...

Six days, six weeks, six months - what was the difference? It was unreal.

The Horror of knowing he was dying.

FROM: Elena PM
TO:Mike Cusnir MD
Wednesday, May 28, 2008 7:52 PM

Dear Dr. Cusnir,
First thanks for all your help and understanding.
A few hours ago we left your office with instructions that I know for sure Francis is not going to follow. I mean:
Drink Tuesday night the bottle with white liquid and fast for Wednesday "scan".
Regarding the food, there is almost nothing he wants or likes. He is by himself in his apt. living miserably.
I'm aware that even with treatment he has not much of life left.
But let's fight for it.
If you could refer him to a "nursing home" starting next Monday and just for the days required until you can perform the relevant tests to determine his condition, treatment options, and so on.
I am willing to help in any capacity.

At the beginning of June I went to visit Francis and found him in very poor physical condition, I called 911. Francis allowed himself to be examined by the paramedics. He was alert, had normal blood pressure, showed no symptoms of urgency and refused to be taken to a hospital, no matter how I asked and insisted. The officer who accompanied the paramedics told me that if I called again for Francis to be taken to a hospital, they would come... but to arrest me. I had no choice but to leave Francis alone with his illness.

Two days later (June 6) he called 911 and was transported to Jackson Memorial Hospital (JMH).

At JMH he was treated professionally. After several tests, I was informed that the cancer (lymphoma) had not metastasized. He was also visited by a doctor in psychiatry who approved my authority as a 'proxy', that allowed me to be informed about all treatment, tests and medications that Francis received.

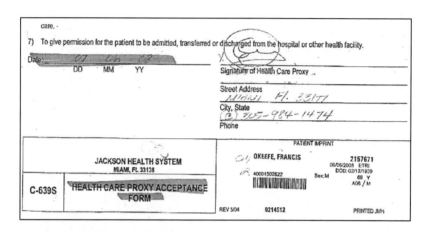

All the miseries that I am going to recount from now on could have been avoided if I had been more alert, better informed, and, if the Health System were not so bureaucratic and mercantile.

On June 13, when we left Jackson Hospital, I didn't know a thing about Hospices and Palliative care. Previously to that day, I had never experienced being totally responsible for someone who was dear to me, and suffered from a terminal illness. However, after seeing all the hardships Francis was subjected to, I ask myself, 'Why didn't I put stop to it?"

Knowing that there was no cure for Francis, I could have brought him to my house where I had a spare room and, where there were three women rotating shifts who, along with taking care of my mother, would also have been able to attend to him. Also, I would have been able to supervise his care and be by his side, instead of driving back and forth from nursing homes and hospitals; all the while discussing and arguing with insensible people about the lack of care he was receiving. What the freaking hell was wrong with me?

Now, I have to live with that painful regret for the rest of my life.

Licenses to Kill

The quality of the health system in South Florida depends on the hospital, the doctor, the rehabilitation center or the hospice. It can go from third-world country care to excellent medical service.There are hospitals and doctors who respect the Hippocratic oath. They provide quality care to patients, with responsible and honest charges for their services. Others show minimal interest in the patient and maximal interest in monetary profits. These are my own conclusions based on personal experience.

What is "palliative sedation"? According to The Journal of the American Medical Association, palliative sedation is the use of sedative medications to relieve extreme suffering by making the patient unaware and unconscious (as in a deep sleep) while the disease takes its course, eventually leading to death. The sedative medication is gradually increased until the patient is comfortable and able to relax. Palliative sedation is not intended to cause death or shorten life.

This is all Francis needed and it was precisely what he never received.

Hospices and nursing homes equal: HELL.

On June 13, Francis was discharged from Jackson Memorial Hospital. The social worker told me about VITAS and contacted the Sales Representative for that institution.

That afternoon, he was transported to Vitas Hospice in Miami Beach. When I got there around 6 p.m. Francis had already been installed in a room where another terminally ill man lay.

VITAS occupied the 6th floor of the building; from the elevator I turned left and walked down a hall which led to five rooms and ended at a reception desk. I heard a woman moaning as I walked down the hall.

There were two black women and a tall black man at the desk.

I: "Good evening. Excuse me, but at one of the rooms down the hall there is a woman moaning."

They: "Yes, we know. And who are you?"

I: "I'm Mr. O'Keefe's friend and proxy. Isn't anyone going to check on this woman?"

The man, who was playing on the computer, stood up unwillingly and said he was going.

I went to Francis's room. A Puerto Rican nurse, I think the only nice person in that merciless place, showed us a resting/dining room where there was a computer which Francis could use.

FROM:francisokeefe@bellsouth.net
TO:epm15@yahoo.com
Friday, June 13, 2008 8:46 PM
Listen to me! The cold is killing me, and I'm not kidding! The jacket I knew that you could not take it. You told me you were to bring me another sweater or not. Well you just call me.   Francis O'Keefe Jr., M.A.

FROM:Elena PM
TO:francisokeefe@bellsouth.net
Saturday, June 14, 2008 8:53 AM
Francis,
I just arrived at work, I'll be here until 6pm.
I need you to inform me of what kind of treatment you get at that center. Medicines, food, hygiene, etc.
I am not pleased at all with that place, but during the weekend we cannot make any changes.Tomorrow I will go to see you and I will bring you some clothes comfortable and warm.
On Monday I will speak with the social worker and I would like to find a nursing home more suitable for you. A kiss, Elena

FROM:francisokeefe@bellsouth.net
TO:epm15@yahoo.com
Get me out of this hospice
Saturday, June 14, 2008 3:33 PM
The cold and pain are driving me crazy. If it were not because they will tie me up and keep me like that for days I would start hitting the walls,
I would have done it! I cannot stand this!
Get me out of this hospice!
Francis O'Keefe Jr., M.A.

Francis's last email.

The hospice was about 25 miles from my job and even further from my house. Nonetheless I went to visit Francis most days. Countless times I tried to talk to him on the phone, but the rabble that worked there transferred all my calls to an unoccupied room. One evening (June 20) I asked a friend to accompany me to visit Francis. I wanted him to witness the situation. Upon exiting the elevator I called from my cell and as we walked through the hall we listened as the phone rang in one of the rooms, but not in that of Francis; I hung up and one minute later I was in front of those people, who were very surprised to see me and said, "But you just called!

"Yes I did," I replied

Among the negligence and abuses I witnessed were that of the woman who complained but no one went to her; and the patient who shared the room with Francis and repeatedly complained of pains in his head but was not ever attended to, at least not while I was there. The three lazy individuals dressed as nurses who were at the reception desk spoke of the visits by a "doctor", whom I never saw. When I spoke with Marla Hoyos and told her about the woman who complained, she said: "Yes, she is always complaining because she wants to have company."

What was that story again about: *To provide comfort and care for patients in the last days of their lives...?*

I am not going to continue providing details of what I saw in that VITAS and the hardships suffered by Francis.

He remained in this detestable hospice for 14 days. – June 13-27.

After much paperwork, on June 27 Francis was transferred to Gramercy Park Nursing Center. VITAS phoned around 6 p.m. to ask me which items belonging to Francis I wanted to be sent. They didn't tell me that Francis had already been sent three hours earlier, nor did they inform me of his condition.

I asked for his wallet, reading glasses, a bottle of Sinex (nasal spray) and three new shirts I had bought days earlier. Nothing I asked was sent; in return I received a pair of shoes and two sweaters that did not belong to Francis. Till the last moment they behaved like the lowlifes they were.

This is a summary of claims processed on 07/07/2008.

PART A - HOSPICE FACILITY CLAIMS

Dates of Service	Services Provided	Amount Charged	Non-Covered Charges	Deductible and Coinsurance	You May Be Billed	See Notes Section
Control number 20818400650305 01						a
Vitas Healthcare Corporation Of						
18001 Old Cutler Road						
Suite 454						
Palmetto Bay, FL 33157-6437						
Referred by: M McBride						
06/13/08-06/30/08	Hospice in hospice facility (Q5006)	$8,665.30	$0.00	$0.00	$0.00	
	Subsequent hospital care (99232)	800.64	0.00	0.00	0.00	
	Hospice in LT/non-skilled NF (Q5003)	557.76	0.00	0.00	0.00	
Claim Total		$10,023.70	$0.00	$0.00	$0.00	

Notes Section:

   a The amount Medicare paid the provider for this claim is $10,023.64.

A bill to Medicare: $715.00 per day!

$10,000 - Ten thousand dollars for 14 days of hell - without medical care and receiving poor nutrition. Besides, there was the psychological abuse of not transferring my calls to Francis, who always needed to talk to me in order not to feel so lonely.

Francis was transferred from VITAS Hospice to the calamitous Gramercy Park Nursing Center, 17475 S. Dixie Highway in Miami. VITAS sent him (about 3:00 pm) to this center in deplorable conditions: dehydrated, vomiting, and with diarrhea. I learned this when I arrived at Gramercy about 8 p.m. Seeing him in that condition, thrown on a bed, I began taking pictures with my cellphone. These are photos that I will never publish for due respect to my dear Francis. The nurses (or whatever these women were), when they saw me taking the photos, became very solicitous and asked what was wrong. I was informed by the nurses that, by orders of Dr. David Goldberg, they had given him something for the vomiting.

I said, "Very good; and what about for the diarrhea? And where is that doctor? It's inadmissible to have this man in this condition. Call now for an ambulance so he can be taken to Jackson South Hospital."

The nurses told me, "That is precisely what they should have done at VITAS, one does not send anyone in that state to a center like this one."

I said,"No, and you don't keep him like that either. Please call an ambulance, now!"

In the meantime they cleaned and changed Francis's bed.

Also, they brought "dinner" for Francis. The ideal diet for a patient with vomiting and diarrhea: Bread with chunks of cheap beef and cold fries.

I do not know what obscure reasons caused these circumstances but the ambulance did not arrive until past midnight. Jackson South Hospital is just five minutes from Gramercy.

Top part of the Admission report where it describes the condition in
which Francis was sent from VITAS to Gramercy Nursing Home.

Botton part of the Discharge report - 8 hours after admission.
"Resident left in stable condition" - I suppose they meant he was still
breathing.

Francis was admitted to Jackson South Hospital (JSH) on the eve of June 28th and discharged on July 1st.

```
***** JACKSON SOUTH COMMUNITY HOSPITAL *****
               9333 S.W. 152ND STREET
                 MIAMI, FLORIDA 33157

                 HISTORY AND PHYSICAL

PATIENT NAME      : OKEEFE,FRANCIS            PATIENT MR # : D296030

DATE OF ADMISSION : 06/28/08                  ACCT # : D83941443

ADMITTING PHYSICIAN: CORONA,ABELARDO          RM #: 218-1


HISTORY OF PRESENT ILLNESS:
The patient is a 69-year-old white male sent in from the nursing home
secondary to intractable nausea, vomiting, diagnosed with gastroenteritis,
volume depletion, renal failure, hyperkalemia.  The patient also found to be
hypotensive.
```

```
DATE OF DISCHARGE: 07/01/08                   RM # :   218-1

PHYSICIAN        : CORONA,ABELARDO




BRIEF SUMMARY AND HOSPITAL COURSE:
This is a 69-year-old white male with past medical history of schizophrenia,
lymphoma, stroke.  The patient presented initially with acute gastroenteritis
along with depletion and hypotension.

The patient responded very well to intravenous fluid hydration at this point
in time.  The patient was initially in Hospice Care; however, the proxy has
disenrolled him in the Hospice.  They wanted a second opinion from an
oncologist at this point in time.  Second opinion has been offered.  There is
no acute intervention at this point in time.

He will need to follow up as an outpatient with Dr. Fine and they will need to
obtain medical records from previous treatment courses, biopsies, pathology
results, and scans.  The patient was transferred over to a Coral Reef Nursing
Home for further monitoring.
```

The Lymphoma was overlooked.
And none of those records were ever obtained.

On July 1st he was transferred to Coral Reef Nursing Home (CRNH).

The only improvement Francis and I had were the locations of the hospital and the nursing home. Both were located on SW 152nd Street, one across from the other, only 10 minutes from my house. This allowed me not only to visit him daily but to keep him company for many hours.

CRNH had a diverse staff. I mean that there were several responsible and caring nurses and their assistants, but also there were a few scoundrels, the main one and the worst of all being the director, Lourdes Morales, an ordinary Cuban woman.

Lourdes Morales
Social Services Director

9869 SW 152nd Street
Miami, FL 33157
Tel: (305).255.3220
Fax: (305).255.1778
Cell: (305).351.6569
lmorales@coralreefnursing.com

Francis once again began to suffer from lack of medical care.

The doctor in charge of Francis had become invisible and there was no way to communicate with him. Nor was I able to communicate with Dr. Flores, the psychiatrist who had medicated Francis with Ziprexa.

On one of my visits I found that Francis had fallen the night before and had banged his head against the floor.

On another occasion I brought him a soda that he liked. He drank half, leaving the rest on the table beside the bed; almost 18 hours later when I returned to visit him again, there was the glass still with soda and Francis lying in bed with pains and malnourished. No one had attended to him.

On the night of July 11th I received a telephone call to inform me that Francis was in lots of pain and they had sent him to JSH. When I arrived the following morning at the hospital, Francis was the same as always: confused and malnourished.

He had refused to have more tests done. I spoke to him and convinced him to allow to be treated. Once again he was stabilized.

At Jackson South Hospital (JSH) Francis had been hospitalized about 13 days earlier with similar symptoms and complaining of the same pains.

Every time Francis was hospitalized I gave verbal information to the doctors about his physical condition, expressly: Terminal Cancer of Lymphoma. Based on all these admission/discharge reports, I have come to the conclusion that there is no communication among the members of the "healthcare system" - hospitals, nursing homes, hospices, doctors - meaning that almost every time one checks in, mainly in a hospital, one has to go through the whole routine of exams, tests, scans, etc. Why can't they check previous records? I don't mean from 10 years before, but from recent hospitalizations, especially when the patient was admitted with the same or similar complaints at the same hospital.

They are extremely efficient when it comes to keep accurate billing records... Can't they do the same with medical records?

PART A HOSPITAL INSURANCE - INPATIENT CLAIMS

Dates of Service		Benefit Days Used	Non-Covered Charges	Deductible and Coinsurance	You May Be Billed	See Notes Section
Control number 20822405733002	01					a
Coral Reef Operating Llc						
Coarl Reef Nursing						
9869 Sw 152nd St						
Miami, FL 33157						
Referred by: Abelardo Corona						
07/04/08-07/22/08		0 days	$5,991.93	$0.00	$0.00	b
Control number 20826202411502	01					c,d,e,
Coral Reef Operating Llc						f
Coarl Reef Nursing						
9869 Sw 152nd St						
Miami, FL 33157						
Referred by: Abelardo Corona						
07/04/08-07/22/08		18 days	$0.00	$0.00	$0.00	

THIS IS NOT A BILL - Keep this notice for your records.

```
***** JACKSON SOUTH COMMUNITY HOSPITAL *****
                9333 S.W. 152ND STREET
                 MIAMI, FLORIDA 33157

                  SHORT STAY SUMMARY

PATIENT NAME    : OKEEFE,FRANCIS              PATIENT MR # : D296030

DATE OF ADMISSION: 07/11/08                   ACCT # : D83963702

DATE OF DISCHARGE: 07/12/08                   RM # : 109-1

PHYSICIAN       : UBEDA,RAFAEL




CHIEF COMPLAINT:
The patient is complaining of abdominal pain and altered mental status.

HISTORY OF PRESENT ILLNESS:
He is a 69-year-old white male, who lives at the Coral Reef Nursing home, with
a history of schizophrenia, abdominal pain, and chronic low back pain, who was
sent by care givers because of altered mental status and abdominal pain,
colicky type, associated with nausea.  No vomiting, no diarrhea, and no
fevers.  The patient takes opioids because of chronic low back pain.  The
patient was evaluated in the emergency room and cleared by psychiatrist and
also by surgeon.

ALLERGIES:
Penicillin.

PAST MEDICAL HISTORY:
Schizophrenia, gastroesophageal reflux, history of coronary artery disease,
and spondylosis.

PAST SURGICAL HISTORY:
Bilateral hernia repairs and carotid endarterectomy.
_____

Denied.

FAMILY HISTORY:
Unremarkable.

REVIEW OF SYSTEMS:
The patient with occasional headaches, relieved spontaneously, and good
appetite, occasional abdominal pain and constipation, also with loose stools.
No melena, no hematochezia, no hematuria.  Low back pain present and weakness

JACKSON SOUTH COMMUNITY HOSP PCI *LIVE* (PCI: OE Database COCDH)

Run: 08/01/08-10:47 by FERGUSON,TAJJII                        Page 1 of 3
```

Dr. Ubeda in this report detailed all but the most important thing: Terminal Lymphoma Cancer. He granted the use of opioids for the relief of back pain; and this poor doctor reported no abnormalities in the abdomen, when in fact by then Francis was beginning to show gray deep spots in the lower abdomen, in addition Francis's complaints of great pain in that area.

And Francis had good appetite… ? Is willing to drink some orange soda good appetite?

Again back to Coral Reef Nursing Home to continue suffering the same negligence by staff and doctors who were supposed to care for him.

Every time I visited Francis, I tried to help him as much as possible. Once I wheeled him out to the garden to converse. Twice he asked if there was no cure. I answered that at the moment," No, but we were keeping him medicated waiting for a new advance of science."

He just remained silent. Also, he once asked about his apartment and his stuff. I told him not to worry; that I was taking care of everything and had already paid the rent for July.

Sunday July 20, I spent most of the day with him. I remember him sitting on the edge of the bed as he asked me, "Elena, do you believe there is life beyond this one?"

"I think so, Francis. I think we have two bodies - one physical/material and one astral/energy." - I said.

F: "Can we make a deal?"

I: "Yes…"

F: "The first of us to leave, will wait for the other."

I: "Yes, Francis."

We sealed the deal with a peck kiss. Maybe it was not the last thing we talked about but, it's the last that I remember of our conversations.

The End of a Life.

All that time that Francis was at the Coral Reef Nursing Home I kept looking for another site to transfer him to. I spoke with Dr. Joaquin Barbara, who once attended to my mother. I explained the situation and the little time of life that Francis had left. Dr.Barbara contacted CRNH; I don't know what agreement they arrived at.
Dr. Barbara worked at Larkin Hospital.

July 22, Tuesday: I was working at West Kendall Regional library when about 6:00 p.m. CRNH called to inform me that Francis had been transferred to Larkin Hospital. I remember I cried, "Great!"

The fact is that anywhere, even under a bridge, was better than that nursing home. Also, Dr. Barbara called me and I remember him saying, "Francis is very ill."

Knowing that Dr. Barbara worked at Larkin made me feel a bit more relaxed about Francis's medical care. --- Wrong assumption !

I informed Ailyn (the inexorable and very religious library manager) of the message from Dr. Barbara, and asked her to authorize me to leave.

She said, "No," and added that if I left three hours early, she would report me and I would be suspended because I had already missed too much time. I was there until 9:00 p.m.; something I will always regret.

I arrived about 10 p.m. at the hospital. Francis was sedated and seemed to be sleeping peacefully.

July 23, 2008

In the morning I phoned my brother Carlos and asked him to pick up our mother. I explained to him that I was staying that night in the hospital with Francis. Then I went to see Dr. Darpini, my physician. I told him about my situation and that I was stressed to the max. He signed an order which certified, effective immediately, that I was to be on leave for 30 days. I arrived at the library wearing blue jeans, handed over the certificate and left to never return to that branch of MDPLS.

Why hadn't I done that a month earlier? Why? Why?

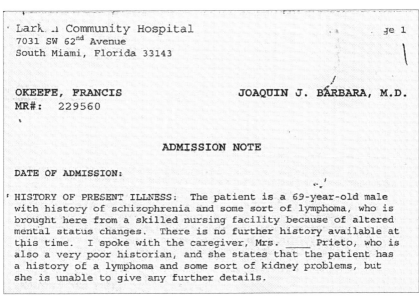

```
Lark  .a Community Hospital                              .a     . ɟe 1
7031 SW 62nd Avenue
South Miami, Florida 33143                                        \


OKEEFE, FRANCIS                       JOAQUIN J. BÁRBARA, M.D.
MR#:   229560


                        ADMISSION NOTE

DATE OF ADMISSION:

HISTORY OF PRESENT ILLNESS:  The patient is a 69-year-old male
with history of schizophrenia and some sort of lymphoma, who is
brought here from a skilled nursing facility because of altered
mental status changes.  There is no further history available at
this time.  I spoke with the caregiver, Mrs. ____ Prieto, who is
also a very poor historian, and she states that the patient has
a history of a lymphoma and some sort of kidney problems, but
she is unable to give any further details.
```

For real, Dr. Barbara? "Some type" of lymphoma? Not a terminal lymphoma cancer, as I had informed you? And I could not give more information? But then, who the hell had I been talking to during the last 15 days about the health and hardships of Francis? I had informed you, and I still have the faxes I sent to your secretary Yanet, that Francis had left little time to live; that I only wanted for him to not suffer anymore. Palliative care!!!

MEDICATIONS: His medication list includes Pepcid 20 mg p.o.
daily, Tylenol 650 mg p.r.n., iron sulfate, Zyprexa 30 mg p.o.
at bedtime, Tigan 200 mg q.6h. p.r.n., _____ p.r.n., Roxanol
p.r.n., Megace, Colace, and clonidine all on a p.r.n. basis.

SOCIAL HISTORY: He apparently lived alone. Now, he is a
skilled nursing facility resident. There is no history of
alcohol or drug abuse available at this time.

PHYSICAL EXAMINATION:
GENERAL: The patient is a very ill looking, cachetic white male
who is poorly responsive to verbal stimuli. He withdraws from
painful stimuli in all four extremities. He looks pale.
HEENT: His oral cavity is dry.
NECK: No JVD.
CHEST: Clear to auscultation bilaterally.
HEART: Heart sounds were with regular rate and rhythm.
Tachycardic. S1 and S2. No S3 or S4. He has sinus rhythm to
130 on telemetry monitor.
ABDOMEN: His abdomen is soft. He is nontender. His bowel
sounds are present. He has got a suprapubic incision that is
well healed.
EXTREMITIES: His lower extremities have no edema.
His Foley has very concentrated and turbid urine.

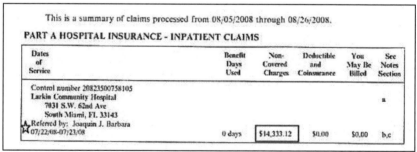

This is a summary of claims processed from 08/05/2008 through 08/26/2008.

PART A HOSPITAL INSURANCE - INPATIENT CLAIMS

Dates of Service	Benefit Days Used	Non-Covered Charges	Deductible and Coinsurance	You May Be Billed	See Notes Section
Control number 20823500758105 Larkin Community Hospital 7031 S.W. 62nd Ave South Miami, FL 33143 Referred by: Joaquin J. Barbara 07/22/08-07/23/08	0 days	$14,333.12	$0.00	$0.00	b,c

Billing for 24 hours of hospitalization: $14,333.

I believe I have the explanation of the erroneous report made by Dr.
Barbara: Simply by not knowing the real condition of Francis, the
doctor could, as he did: order all kinds of tests, X-rays, scans,etc.
Because that's where the Almighty Dollar is. Amen.

I arrived at Larkin hospital at noon. Francis had been all this time in the emergency area, in a room for a single patient. He was half asleep, I took a chair and sat beside him. His hands were cold. At one point I heard him complain; I left the room and asked urgently to put him on morphine.

Before that I had spoken softly in his ear, "Francis, I'm here and I'll be with you always until the end of life.

I believed then that the end of life was going to come in a few days, during which time I was going to be near him all that time. But that was not going to be the case.

He was dying. I learned that when a nurse came to check the IV fluids and I asked her what was it for, to which she answered, "to keep his blood pressure up."

"And what will happen if you disconnect it?" I asked.

"He will die soon," she replied.

I looked at a helpless Francis for a few seconds and I said to the nurse, "Do it, please."

She shut off the IV and left the room. I stayed there, holding his hand, looking at him and not knowing what to think or feel. The nurse came back and told me not to hold Francis's hand, that it sometimes delays the end.

I dropped his hand, but a minute later I took it again. Something told me that he needed to feel my presence. On the wall there was a clock.

Suddenly Francis took a breath, and then one more, for the last time. It was 5:57 p.m., 23 July, 2008. I stayed sitting next to him with tears in my eyes and saying to myself, "...and this is all."

I left the room and reported it to the nurses, who ran into the room to take his vital signs. As I was walking toward the exit, I heard one of them saying, "How come? He was scheduled for a scan first thing in the morning!"

I kept walking and with a sad smile I thought: Sorry bitch, but this time we beat you.

I went out to the street to smoke a cigarette and to look up to the sky. Francis was now on his way up to a much better life, or at least I want to believe that, where he will wait for me if, he can forgive me for being so stupid that I failed him when he needed me the most .

```
Larkin Community Hospital                              Page 1
7031 SW 62nd Avenue
, South Miami, Florida 33143
                                                        7|23

OKEEFE, FRANCIS                    JOAQUIN J. BARBARA, M.D.
MR#:  229560


                        EXPIRATION

DATE OF ADMISSION:  07/22/2008

DATE OF DISCHARGE:  07/23/2008

ADMITTING DIAGNOSES:
1.    Metabolic acidosis.
2.    Acute renal failure.
3.    Lymphoma.

HISTORY:  The patient was a 69-year-old male, who was admitted
through the emergency room from Coral Reef Nursing Home with the
diagnosis of altered mental status changes.  In the emergency
room, he was found to be severely acidotic.  He was given 2 amps
of sodium bicarbonate by the emergency room physician in that he
was aggressively hydrated.  On admission, he was found to have a
creatinine of 3.5.  In his KUB, he had evidence of bilateral J-
stents previously placed.  The patient was admitted to the
intensive care unit where he was again aggressively hydrated,
and morphine sulfate was used to control his pain.  Caregiver
was at the bedside and she stated that the patient had
previously been on hospice and did not want any aggressive
measure to further prolong the patient's life unnecessarily.
The patient remained hypotensive throughout the day today and
expired at 1810, with his caregiver at the bedside.



JJB:emt7753 05335177
D:07/23/2008 22:10          _____
T:07/24/2008 03:03          JOAQUIN J. BARBARA; M.D.
```

Days later, after midnight the phone rang; no one calls me so late, except Francis. So, the first thing I thought of was - Francis - understanding immediately that it could not be him. I went back to sleep crying.

The Apartment

How sad it is to close the last home of someone so dear! While cremation was being resolved, I went for three consecutive days to his apartment to liquidate his belongings. It hurt to see and touch his clothes (some unworn), the two bikes tied in the parking lot, his computer, his drawings and even his medications.

The first thing I did was to open all the drawers and put in plastic bags all the papers I found written by him, as well as cassettes and discs; everything that had his writing or his voice recorded. I brought home all the bags. Also, I brought his toolbox and other small things: I call them my inheritance.

A neighbor of his opened the computer and removed the hard drive, which I destroyed as best I could, not wanting for anyone to have access to Francis's files.

Once home, I gave myself the task of reviewing the more than 15 bags of papers, the vast majority totally illegible. Among disks and papers I found many of the testimonies that I have presented in this book.

After reviewing all, I built an oven with four concrete blocks in my yard and burned everything else. I could not trash his stuff.

O'Keefe's Relatives

The night that Francis died I made arrangements by telephone with Vior Funeral Home. They would be responsible for collecting the body at Larkin hospital and proceeding with the cremation within 48 hours. Then I was to receive the urn and death certificate. The cost: $800. Very well, I was to go by the funeral home in the morning to sign the papers and pay. Nothing complicated, right? Sad, yes, but not complicated.

I will simplify the story: At the funeral home I was greeted by Jorge Rivero, the director. We talked about all the things concerning the matter, and then he said, "You know, you cannot order the cremation of Mr. O'Keefe."

"Why?" I asked.

"If you are not a family member, the law will not allow it."

"What you do then?" I asked.

"Does he have any relatives?"

"Actually, no," I answered.

"In that case, you need the authorization of a judge. You need to go to the courthouse downtown."

"Well, I will do that," I said.

The reality was that Mr. Rivero was not fully versed with all the regulations and laws of the funeral system, and that morning he himself invented such "authorization of a judge."

There is a State of Florida Statute that had allowed me to authorize the cremation.

surrogate of the dead person at the time of death, a public health officer, the medical examiner, county commission, or administrator acting under part II of chapter 406 or other public administrator; a representative of a nursing home or other health care institution in charge of final disposition or a friend or other person not listed in this subsection who is willing to assume the responsibility as the legally authorized person. Where there is a person in any priority class listed in this subsection, the funeral establishment shall rely upon the authorization of any one legally authorized person of that class if that person represents that she or he is not aware of any objection to the cremation of the deceased's human remains by others in the same class of the person making the representation or of any person in a higher priority class.

Florida Statute 497

That day (July 24, 2008) began an unnecessary torment for me that lasted until November 5.

     * I visited the court, going from one floor to another, as no one had any idea of what I needed.
     * I asked lawyers I met in the corridors. Nothing!
     * I visited the Legal Aid Society. Nothing!
     * I contacted the Cuban American Bar Association. Nothing!
     * I visited the Miami-Dade County Medical Examiner - the Morgue Bureau. Nothing!

Medical Examiner   Page 1

Miami-Dade County
Medical Examiner

Website and content provided by Miami-Dade County

Public Interment Program

The purpose of the Public Interment Program (PIP) is to provide final disposition in accordance with the law for those persons who have no family or cannot afford private funeral arrangements. In order to qualify for this program, the death must have occurred within Miami-Dade County (even though the decedent may not have been a County resident), and the decedent must be declared indigent or unclaimed. A decedent is considered indigent if his/her financial status is unknown or if the next of kin is financially unable to arrange for final disposition. A decedent is considered unclaimed if the next of kin cannot be located, or, if located, do not accept responsibility for the final disposition.

Then I thought maybe there might be some relative of Georgia O'Keeffe who was still alive. I went to Google and spent one hour searching.

Looking at a genealogy chart, the only persons that might possibly be still alive were June and Catherine. I had to take into consideration that the vast majority of U.S. citizens use only a paternal surname, and most women take the surname of their spouses.

So what were their names? Finally, I found the grand-nephew of Georgia: Raymond R. Krueger, a lawyer established in Wisconsin.

I telephoned his office. He took my call and I briefly explained the situation.

He had to talk to June, Francis's cousin, who in this case was the closest relative. After this an exchange of emails and phone conversations began between June Sebring and Raymond Krueger.

FROM: epm15@yahoo.com TO: rrkruger@michaelbest.com Tuesday, July 29, 2008 12:46 PM	FROM: June Sebring TO: epm15@yahoo.com CC: Krueger, Raymond R. Friday, August 8, 2008 12:46 PM

Many of the documents I have presented in this book were sent to them by emails, which I have all saved, and/or fax. But it was not enough. They began to doubt that *"this individual is our distant relative, known as Francis."* They insisted that I take a picture of the body; also that I obtain a copy of Francis's fingerprints from the U.S. Armed Forces and have them compared with those on record at the police department to verify the identity of the body.

Excuse me, but I was a Public Library employee, not a C.I.A. agent.

The days passed and nothing got resolved. In the meantime I was wasting my time and money. Mr. Rivero kept calling me on the phone constantly demanding that I solve the problem; Francis in a freezer was a daily expenditure of $200, etc., etc.

Finally my good friend and journalist Pedro Yanes connected me with The Miami Herald. Reporter Daniel Shoer Roth was commissioned to write the article.

Jorge Rivero (Vior Funeral) phoned me and threatened to sue me if The Herald published something negative about him or his funeral home. At that moment I was not aware that all that mess was a product of his "authorization by a judge" invention.

The Herald article provided us with a minute of fame, but everything remained the same. Pedro Yanes recommended me to a lawyer friend of his, Leonardo Viota Sesin, who kindly made several efforts *pro bono*, but couldn't go much farther.

Eventually, Mr. Krueger and Ms. Sebring concluded by washing their hands. They never accepted the identity of Francis, responded to my last email, nor answered telephone calls from Vior Funeral Home or those of the Miami Herald reporter.

Ultimately, I came to think that what really concerned these relatives was that perhaps I could make monetary claims. Years ago, after the death of Georgia, there was a dispute for the inheritance.

In the New York Times, July 1987: *"Settlement is granted over O'Keeffe estate. The dispute involved her will, executed in 1979, and two amendments in 1983 and 1984. The entire estate was valued at $65 million."*

Francis, as the only nephew of Georgia, had every right to claim part of that fortune but, already schizophrenic and a vagabond, did not make any claim.

Finally, Mr. Rivero found the above-mentioned Statute 497-37, and asked me to go to the funeral home to sign the papers, saying that it was OK to proceed with the cremation. However, I returned to the medical examiner and showed a copy of the statute to the director, who gave me a verbal approval. On Wednesday, November 5, 2008, Francis was cremated, exactly 15 weeks after his death.

ABCO
820 Northwest 57th Street
Fort Lauderdale, Florida 33309

I hereby certify that herein are contained the Cremated Remains

of: **FRANCIS WYCKOFF OKEEFE**

Cremated on the _____ 5th day of November, 2008

Permit No. _____ 3435 _____ County of Death _____ Miami-Dade

Date of Death _____ 23rd day of July, 2008

Funeral Firm _____ VIOR FUNERAL HOME

ABCO

By: _____
Crematory Representative

IN MEMORIAM

FRANCIS WYCKOFF O'KEEFE, JR.
1939 - 2008
A very intelligent, difficult, but
most of all a very good man.
Love always, Elena

Ashes

A few days later being all by myself at home I placed the urn on a table, lighted a candle, placed Francis's photo next to it, and played the cassette with our recorded voices conversing and singing; those were some of the best times that we shared during our 10 years of a very special friensdship.

Looking and holding that box which contains the body of a human being turned into ashes was and is a surrealistic experience.

Weird thoughts came to my mind : I kept thinking about his blue eyes. I haven't dare to open the box to see his ashes; one day I will.

I can look at his photos and at his handwritten notes; I can listen to his voice in our recordings and although sadly I can still smile, but the urn with his ashes is beyond me.

When I die my family has the instructions to throw our ashes together at sea.

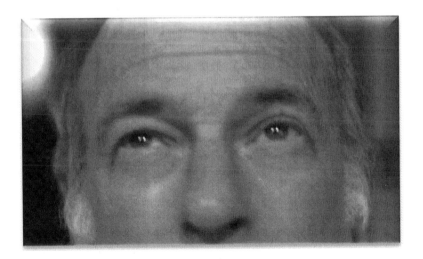

Elena PM

Epilogue

I'd like to offer my gratitude to all those people who, at any time during Francis's life, did for him an act of kindness, offered him assistance, greeted him in a friendly manner, or just treated him with the respect he deserved.

I'd like to say to all those people who despised and/or mistreated Francis O'Keefe, Jr. that Francis was always morally and culturally far above all of you put together. You people are trash and the type that's not even good for recycling.

Francis:

I remember that once when talking to you - for the hundredth time - about "the book", you, smiling, said, "Elena, you are never going to write that book."

It has taken me 18 years and 18 million tears but "a promise is a debt."

I want and need to believe that there is another dimension in which you exist, free of all the afflictions you suffered here; and keeping all the good that was in you - your intelligence, your joy and your nobility.

I love you and miss you, Mr. F. O'K.

Always, Elena

Fin

About the Author

(October 2016 - Photographer: CAP)
Elena PM
(Elena Prieto-Miranda)

A tattered, four-decade-old copy of a handwriting analysis produced for Elena revealed these truths:
"Phonies irritate you."
"You loathe restrictions and must have complete independence."
"You are satisfied and fond of the simple things in life."

Elena, citizen of the world as she describes herself, has mixed feelings about humankind.

One of her most favorite book is "Jonathan Livingston Seagull."
And her favorite sculpture Le Penseur / The Thinker.

As an atheist, Elena firmly believes that:
"The power to question is the basis of all human progress."
-Indira Gandhi

On the reverse of this medallion is engraved her motto:
"Be Good - Be Wise - Be Yourself."

Made in the USA
Middletown, DE
19 August 2022

71630294R00102